AF559685

Memorable Quotes from
Rajiv Gandhi
and
on
Rajiv Gandhi

ABOUT THE COMPILER

Prof. Ganapathi Palanithurai, Coordinator in Rajiv Gandhi Chair, Gandhigram Rural Institute, presently heads the Department of Political Science and Development Administration, Gandhigram Rural University, Tamil Nadu. He is also Associated with Centre Planning Commission, State Planning Commission ofTamil Nadu, Population Foundation of India, the Ford Foundation, UNICEF, Rajiv Gandhi Foundation, CAPART, Ministry of Rural Development and DANIDA (Danish-Indo Development Agency) in specific areas of activities in connection with empowerment of people.

Prof. Palanithurai has to his credit fifty-two books and ninty-five articles on three major areas, namely, legislative behaviour, ethnicity and Panchayati Raj system. He was recipient of Fellowship from Sastri Indo-Canadian Institute, New Delhi and World Academy of Art and Science, USA. He is the Chairman of the Tamil Nadu Council for Sustainable Livelihoods. He was a visiting Fellow in the MiGill University, Canada in 1989. He is a member of the expert committee constituted by the Government of Tamil Nadu to monitor the training programme for local body leaders. He is a member of High Level Committee headed by the Minister of Panchayati Raj, Government of Tamil Nadu for further devolution of powers.

Memorable Quotes from RAJIV GANDHI and on RAJIV GANDHI

Compiled by
G. Palanithurai

Foreword by
Shri Mani Shankar Aiyar

CONCEPT PUBLISHING COMPANY, NEW DELHI–110059

ISBN-13: 978-81-8069-587-2 **ISBN-10: 81-8069-587-5**

First Published 2009

Published and Printed by

Concept Publishing Company

Regd. Office:

A/15-16, Commercial Block, Mohan Garden

New Delhi-110059 (India)

Phones : 25351460, 25351794, *Fax* : 091-11-25357109

Email : publishing@conceptpub.com,
website: www.conceptpub.com

Editorial Office:

H-13, Bali Nagar, New Delhi-110 015, India.

Cataloging in Publication Data--*Courtesy:* D.K. Agencies (P) Ltd. <docinfo@dkagencies.com>

Memorable quotes from Rajiv Gandhi and on Rajiv Gandhi / compiled by G. Palanithurai ; foreword by Mani Shankar Aiyar.

p. cm.

ISBN 13: 9788180695872 ISBN 10: 8180695875

1. Gandhi, Rajiv, 1944-1991--Quotations. 2. Prime ministers--India--Quotations. 3. India--Politics and government--1977- --Quotations, maxims, etc. I. Gandhi, Rajiv, 1944-1991. II. Palanithurai, G. (Ganapathy), 1953-

DDC 954.052 22

To
The Divine Mother

FOREWORD

Much as I am tempted to write a long foreword to this compilation of selected quotations from the speeches of Prime Minister Rajiv Gandhi, I am restraining myself from doing so because I thought his words should be allowed to speak for themselves.

Instead, let me quote a few key extracts from my tribute to him in my maiden speech in Parliament in the aftermath of the shock wave that hit me when he was assassinated on 21 May 1991 on his way to canvass for me in my constituency. My speech focused on the four pillars of this policy: Democracy, Socialism, Secularism and Non-alignment, the themes that pervaded the thousand or more speeches he made during his Prime Ministership, in many of which I had a small part to play.

I said then, and I reiterate now:

"He believed deeply in our ***democracy****. He believed that our democracy, as it now exists, is flawed because it is a superstructure without a sound basis, And he toiled towards establishing that sound foundation for our* ***democracy****."*

The Panchayati Raj revolution sweeping through rural

India is, in the scale and scope of its operation, without precedent in world history and without parallel in the contemporary world. Constitutional Panchayati Raj owes its flowering to Rajiv Gandhi.

> *"He believed deeply in our* **socialism,** *not perhaps the socialism of the well-known text-books, but a socialism based upon concern for the common man, a socialism based upon using the gifts of knowledge, of science and technology for the advancement of the humblest and the poorest."*

In the full flush of our recent trajectory of growth, and the inequalities in income and wealth that this has generated, the time is apposite to remind ourselves of what socialism meant to Rajiv Gandhi.

> *"His was a profound belief in* **secularism.** *Our secularism, as he saw it, was a celebration of all that is great in India, and what he saw great in India was not simply political entities which we today call the Union of India, but an ideas, a concept, of the celebration of diversity. That is why he has in all the different foods of India, and in all the different languages of India, in all the different cultures of India, in all the different religions of India, in all the different trends of thoughts and schools of opinion that exist in this country."*

That was before the wanton destruction of the Babri

Masjid challenged the national ideology of unity in diversity.

"He recognised, as perhaps no Indian did, that the period of détente made Non-alignment more relevant than it has ever been because the ultimate purpose of Non-alignment is to put an end to the quest for dominance and that quest for dominance has not ended merely because there is a détente between the two superpowers."

Of those two superpowers that existed in July 1991 when I spoke, one – the Soviet Union – was set to disappear into history just two months later. In the world that remains, the quest for dominance has assumed an even sharper edge. A multi-polar world cannot be achieved without blunting the edge of the quest for dominance.

This compilation of extracts from his speeches reminds us of the India of Rajiv Gandhi's dreams. All of us who are inheritors of the Rajiv Gandhi legacy must welcome Prof. G. Palanithurai's heroic effort to retrieve those dreams from the past and bring them to the attention of a new generation of readers. I extend to him my congratulations and my deep gratitude.

Mani Shankar Aiyar

New Delhi
24 July 2008

ACKNOWLEDGEMENTS

Whenever I speak in public fora, I have the habit of quoting extensively from Rajiv Gandhi's observations about events and issues and explaining his perspectives on democracy, development, gender, inclusion and so on. Many friends, after listening to me, have often asked me where I got these gems of utterances. I used to tell them that they were all from various published materials on Rajiv Gandhi. Then they suggested to me to bring out a compilation of memorable quotes of Rajiv Gandhi. When I saw a book published by Concept Publishing Company containing random thoughts of Mahatma Gandhi, I was reminded of my friends' suggestion. So, when Mr. Ashok Kumar Mittal of Concept Publishing Company requested me to compile the notable utterances of Rajiv Gandhi, I took it up very seriously. The result is this compilation. I express my deep sense of gratitude to the many who constantly helped me to give my best to society. The list starts from my parents and includes many from all walks of life. It is just impossible to make everyone of them. Hence, I express my sincere thanks to all those who have helped me directly and indirectly in all my endeavours.

G. Palanithurai

PREFACE

Statesmen are always determined to see the distant future perspicaciously and mould society accordingly. They always lead the society and are never led by the masses. They are visionaries who generate projections. These are expressed and their followers are expected to translate them into action. Their thoughts are expressed in many fora. They are recorded and revisited for introspection and emulation. In this regard, Rajiv Gandhi is a remarkable leader of this century. His prophetic vision and foresightedness have made India strong today. In one of his speeches he observed: "We have missed the Industrial Revolution, but we cannot miss the IT Revolution." Now we realize how intuitively and futuristically he perceived the implications of IT in today's world. On another occasion he said that technology is an imperative for alleviating poverty, that improved technologies alone can help the poor and that unless the poor and technology are integrated, we cannot reduce poverty. While analyzing the speeches of Rajiv Gandhi, one cannot but must be struck by the depth and perspicacity of his mind. It is unfortunate that we lost such a prophetic leader prematurely. It is a loss not only to India but also to the entire continent. During his tenure as Prime Minister of India, he took steps to sow the seeds of prosperity and to unleash the potential of India. He had a dream of leading India to the twenty first century. It is his vision that is being realized today. To the world he showed the face of his grandfather Nehru, the statesman, and to the people of India he showed the face of Nehru, the humanitarian visionary. He developed a framework for deepening democracy and achieving development. His passion for inclusive growth, development and democracy is embedded in his numerous speeches. Since it is not easy for an ordinary person to go through all the speeches of Rajiv Gandhi, I felt that a compilation of his notable thoughts and utterances carefully chosen to capture his perspective would be handy. Hence this compilation of memorable quotes from Rajiv Gandhi's speeches.

CONTENTS

*Foreword by **Shri Mani Shankar Aiyar*** vii

Acknowledgements x

Preface xi

Section – I

1. Activating Panchayats 3
2. Administration Stagnant 4
3. Advantage of North 5
4. A New World Order 6
5. A Plea to give Power to the People 7
6. A Responsive Administration 8
7. A Right Value System 9
8. Balanced Growth 10
9. Building a Casteless Society 11
10. Catch the IT Bus 12
11. Celebrating Diversity 13
12. Centre-State Relations 14
13. Change with times 15
14. Combating Communalism 16
15. Compartmentalization of India 17
16. Constitutionalisation of Grassroots Democracy 18
17. Containing Communalism 19
18. Cooperatives for the Poor 20
19. Country We Want to Build 21
20. Critical Mass will do Critical Function 22
21. Defaulting Mind 23

CONTENTS

22. Defective Educational System 24
23. Democracy and Development 25
24. Dialectics of Secularism 26
25. Dignity of the House 27
26. Disciplining 28
27. District Administration not a Representative 29
28. Earth Citizen 30
29. Education for Thinking 31
30. Education in Our Daily Life 32
31. Education is a Great Equalizer 33
32. Education is Nation Building 34
33. Efficient Public Sector 35
34. End Communal Forces 36
35. Entry to Politics 37
36. Environment and Development 38
37. Extension Work by Men 39
38. Farmers Our Backbone 40
39. Fighting Communalism and Terrorism 41
40. First Man to Think this Issue 42
41. Freedom and Responsibility 43
42. Free People 44
43. Gandhiji's Dream 45
44. Gap between People and Government 46
45. Give Power to the People 47
46. Goals of Education 48
47. Good Must be United 49
48. Good Neighbours 50
49. Grassroots Ignored in Reform 51
50. Human Resource Development 52
51. Human Unity 53
52. I have a Dream 54
53. Idea comes through a Process 55

CONTENTS

54. Implications of Mass Movements 56
55. Importance of Dialogue 57
56. Importance of Traditional Values 59
57. Improving Education 60
58. India and China Relations 61
59. India Demonstrated 62
60. India had a Tradition of Panchayats 63
61. India is Immortal 64
62. India is Not Ordinary Nation 65
63. India is Second to None 66
64. India is Strong 67
65. Indian Approach to Indian Problem 68
66. Indian Unity is Strength 69
67. Indian Women 70
68. India's Heritage 71
69. India's Nationalism 72
70. India's Pluralism 73
71. India's Progress is Felt 74
72. Indigenous Base of Science and Technology 75
73. Japan's Uniqueness 76
74. Life Long Education 77
75. Linkage between Poverty and Technology 78
76. Linking Technology with Farmers 79
77. Local Body is People's Rights 80
78. Mainstreaming Women 81
79. Make India a Model 82
80. Make Power Brokers Out 83
81. Man with Modern Technology 84
82. Mandate for Unity and Strength 85
83. Mass Education 86
84. Mind and Matter 87
85. Missing Concern for Environment 88

CONTENTS

86. Modernity and Tradition 89
87. Need of Change in Educational System 90
88. Need of Opposition 91
89. Need of Reform in Administration 92
90. Need of Reform in Education 93
91. Nehru Stood for Democracy 94
92. New Theory in Democracy 95
93. New Theory of Indian Democracy 96
94. Not People's Fault 97
95. Objectives of Education 98
96. Our Administrative Maladies 99
97. Our Administrative System 100
98. Our Experience in Grassroots Democracy 101
99. Our Politics 102
100. Our Science and Technology 103
101. Our System of Democracy 104
102. Our Wealth 105
103. Panchayats and Social Justice 106
104. Panchayats on their Own Feet 107
105. Panditji and Panchayati Raj 108
106. Participatory Growth and Democracy 109
107. Patriotism 110
108. Pen has Lost its Strength 111
109. People are Always Secular 112
110. People is Our Wealth 113
111. People's Faith in Our Democracy 114
112. Perception on Bureaucracy 115
113. Perfection for Professionalism 116
114. Plan without People's Participation 117
115. Planning from Below 119
116. Poverty Reduction 120
117. Power of Indian Youth 121

118. Power to People 122
119. Process of National Integration 123
120. Public Awareness 124
121. Public Sector 125
122. Quality and People Centric Education 126
123. Recapture the Spirit of India 127
124. Reform our Administrative System 128
125. Reforming Elections 129
126. Religion is Personal 130
127. Remembering Gandhiji 131
128. Reservation of Seats for SC/ST and Imperative 132
129. Responsive Administration 133
130. Role of Centre and State in Strengthening Panchayats 134
131. Role of Power Brokers 135
132. Role of Press in Combating Communalism 136
133. Roots of Democracy Strengthened 137
134. Rural-Urban Continuum 138
135. Safeguarding our Freedom 139
136. Science and Environment 140
137. Science for Everyday Life 141
138. Scientific Temper 142
139. Scientific Temper 143
140. Secular Credentials of India 144
141. Secular Culture 146
142. Secular India 147
143. Secularism 148
144. Self-Reliant Industries 149
145. Separating Religion and Politics 150
146. Skill Upgradation 151
147. Social Justice for Democracy 152
148. Spirit of India 153

149. Spirit of Sacrifice 154
150. Spiritualism is Our Strength 155
151. Strength of India 156
152. Strengthening Democracy 157
153. Strengthening the Panchayati Raj System 158
154. Struggle for Human Rights 159
155. Struggle for Water but Mismanaging Water 160
156. Subjugation of Scientific Tradition 161
157. Systematic Solution 162
158. Tackling Communalism 163
159. Taking India to New Heights 164
160. Technology and Development 165
161. Technology for Today 166
162. The New Education has a Goal 167
163. Top Strong Bottom Weak 168
164. Training 169
165. Tribute to Two Gandhians 170
166. Truly Responsible Administration 171
167. Trusting People 172
168. 21st Century India 173
169. Unique Educational System 174
170. Unique University 175
171. United India 176
172. Unity and Integrity 177
173. Uphold the Unity of India 178
174. Uplifting Women – A Precondition for Development 179
175. Value System in India 180
176. Variations in Devolution 181
177. We are Capable but Restraint 182
178. We are for Humanity Development 183
179. We Need Quick Action 184

180. Weak Structure of Our Democracy 185
181. Where are Harijans in Panchayats? 186
182. Where is women in Governance? 187
183. Women to be Empowered 188
184. Women Under-represented 189
185. Women with Moral Strength 190
186. Work for Unity 191

Section – II

1. A Free Thinker 195
2. A Man who Stood Tall 196
3. A New Era 197
4. A Statesman 198
5. An Innovative Parliamentarian 199
6. An Outstanding Democrat 200
7. Betrayal Tolerated 201
8. Committed for Decentralization 202
9. Concern for Depressed Class 203
10. Constitutional Reformer 204
11. Decency and Fair Play 205
12. Deep Commitment in International Affairs 206
13. Determined Endeavour 207
14. Eminent Parliamentarian 208
15. Foresighted Visionary 209
16. Forthrightness 210
17. Gave New Impetus to SAARC 211
18. Gem among the Jewels 212
19. Good Listener 213
20. Great Son of India 214
21. His Greatest Contribution 215

22. In Support of Peoples Struggle 216
23. Insight 217
24. International Statesman 218
25. Invincible for the Opposition 220
26. Leader of the Third World 221
27. Left on Intelligible Mark 222
28. Modern National Architect 223
29. Nationalist Parliamentarian 224
30. New Style of Confrontation 226
31. Non-Violence 227
32. Prince Among the Politicians 228
33. Rare Among Rarest 229
34. Right Successor 230
35. Shadow Cabinet 231
36. Statesman of Excellent Calibre 232
37. Stood for High Principles 233
38. Stood for Secularism 234
39. True heir of Nehru 235
40. World Leader 236
41. Youngest Leader 236

Section – I

ACTIVATING PANCHAYATS

"The community must decide for itself what activity would be beneficial to it; what are the things that the Central Government must do, what the State governments must do, what can be taken up at the district level, and most important, what are the things that the people must themselves do through the panchayats. It is clear that until panchayats are activated they will continue to lack strength, notwithstanding all the conferences we may hold, all the speeches we may make here in the cities."

Source: Inaugural address to the 13th All India Panchayat Parishad, New Delhi, 22nd September, 1986.

ADMINISTRATION STAGNANT

"The world is changing much too fast for us to have a moribund system which is non-flexible, which cannot evolve and develop with changes in our society, in our country, as they come about in the world."

Source: Inaugural Speeches at the Workshops of District Collectors and Magistrates on Responsive Administration, Jaipur, 30th April, 1988.

ADVANTAGE OF NORTH

"By achieving the industrial revolution earlier than us, the countries of the North today command the lion's share of global resources. They use their technological superiority and command over resources to perpetuate their near monopoly over research, information and the media of communication. Their research is undertaken in the perspective of their own problems. Their relative unfamiliarity with the complex problems of developing societies often leads them down the wrong path of prescribing thing which are frequently irrelevant and sometimes inimical to our concerns and interests."

Source: Speech at the Second Conference of Research Information System for Non-Aligned and Other Developing Countries, New Delhi, 20th November, 1985.

A NEW WORLD ORDER

"The quest for dominance is a condition of mind. It is that mindset which seizes upon the problems of others to expand its sphere of influence through interference or intervention which seeks solutions to specific situations in terms of extraneous interests, which perpetuates a world power structure that denies the common humanity of humankind. It is that mindset which has to be metamorphosed. It is that mindset which has to be converted to the principles and perceptions of our vision of the world. It is that mindset which has to be persuaded of the need for the true democratization of the world order. The unity of human family has to be affirmed even as the diversity of human civilization is cherished and celebrated. That in sum, must be the Non-aligned Movement's task for the future."

Source: Prime Minister Rajiv Gandhi's address to the Ninth Non-Aligned Summit at Belgrade on 5th September, 1989.

A PLEA TO GIVE POWER TO THE PEOPLE

"We invite all the Parties in the House to join hands with us in passing these Bills. The Bills are for the people. The Bills are for their welfare, their benefit. The Bills are to end the reign of the power-brokers. The Bills are to entrust responsibility to the grassroots. The Bills are to give responsive administration. The Bills are to involve the people's participation in the planning and implementation of development and social justice. The Bills are designed to entrench democracy in the very foundations of our polity...The Bills represent the realisation of Mahatma Gandhiji's vision. The bills represent the fulfilment of Pandit Jawaharlal Nehru's dream. The Bills are the outgrowth of Indiraji's endeavours."

Source : Mani Shankar Aiyar, "Rajiv Gandhi in Parliament" in *Rajiv Gandhi and Parliament* (ed.) C.K. Jain, New Delhi: CBS Publishers and Distributors, 1992, p. 134.

A RESPONSIVE ADMINISTRATION

"A responsive administration is tested most at the point of interface between the administration and the people."

Source: Inaugural Speeches at the Workshops of District Collectors and Magistrates on Responsive Administration, Hyderabad, 13th February, 1988.

A RIGHT VALUE SYSTEM

"A right value system must be built into our education system. We must be very clear that religion and politics must be separated and there must be a very clear definition of the difference between spirituality of the religion and its rituals and dogmas. We must be clear that secularism as we understand it is not anti-religion or non-religion, it is only the separation of government from religion. Religion has a great role to play in the development process of our nation and we should do nothing to undermine that."

Source: Speech while inaugurating a Science and Technology Institute after visiting the Adiparasakthi Temple, Meelmaruvathur, Tamil Nadu, 12th November, 1988.

BALANCED GROWTH

"We must see that regional imbalances in the growth of various parts of the country are removed and all the states progress evenly. We shall ensure that all citizens of the country get full opportunity to contribute their might towards India's progress."

Source: Independence Day speech from the ramparts of Red Fort, 15th August, 1985.

BUILDING A CASTELESS SOCIETY

"The second point which must be a part of the national goal, is a casteless society. The Constitution very clearly differentiates between Scheduled Castes and Backward Classes. Why did our Constitution makers make this distinction? They had something in their mind. Why have we lost that distinction today? I agree with you that reality is that caste accounts for a tremendous amount in this country. I do not disagree with that. But what is our goal? Is our goal a casteless society? If our goal is a casteless society, surely every step that we take must be towards that objective."

Source: Vasanth Sathe, "Rajiv Gandhi and Parliament" in *Rajiv Gandhi and Parliament* (ed.) C.K. Jain, New Delhi: CBS Publishers and Distributors, 1992, p. 239.

CATCH THE IT BUS

"India missed the Industrial Revolution, it cannot afford to miss the Computer Revolution."

Source: Ranbir Singh and M. Khosla, *Rajiv Gandhi: The Man, the Pilot, the Politician*, 1992, p. 50.

CELEBRATING DIVERSITY

"...Economic opportunity has opened the door to unprecedented mobility for our population. This mobility is uprooting millions from traditional cultural moorings. Many millions more than ever before are interacting at a personal level with people of different languages, of different cultures and of different faiths. For all of them we must make our diversity a living reality. Our education system is being improved to inculcate the right values. Our seven Zonal Cultural Centres are taking the message of diversity to the people at their door-steps doing commendable work in remote and far-flung areas in city slums and in small towns of bringing people together from every corner of the country and bringing the culture of different parts of the country together."

Source: L.S. Deb, 22nd January, 1985, c. 319.

CENTRE-STATE RELATIONS

"Our attitude to Centre-State relations is based on Gandjij's view. At the Round Table Conference in 1931, Gandhiji described the Congress in the following terms. I quote "It is what it means—national. It represents no particular community, no particular class, no particular interest. It claims to represent all the Indian interests and all classes." He went on to add: "Above all, the Congress represents, in it essence, the dumb, semi-starved millions scattered over the length and breadth of the land in its 700,000 villages... Every interest which, in the opinion of Congress, is worthy of protection, has to sub-serve the interests of those dumb millions; and so you do find now and again apparently a clash between several interests. But if there is a genuine real clash, I have no hesitation in saying on behalf of the Congress that the Congress will sacrifice every interest for the sake of the interests of these dumb millions..""

Source: Excerpts from the reply in Lok Sabha to the debate on the President's Address, 3rd March, 1989.

CHANGE WITH TIMES

"Our Plans cannot be hard and dogmatic. They must change with the times and move with the development of our country. Every year brings new compulsions, new circumstances, and with each Plan these must be taken into consideration."

Source: Intervention in Rajya Sabha during the discussion on the Seventh Plan, 17th December, 1985.

COMBATING COMMUNALISM

"The minorities too have their own problems and we have to give them special attention. But the one predominant problem is that of communalism. We have to combat it fully, steadfastly. If there is one thing that weakens India, it is communalism. If we do not combat and end communalism, it will gnaw at the country's vital and destroy us. We have to ensure that all forces in India unite to combat communalism. No corner of the country is to be left our; there must be no weakening in fighting communalism."

Source: Free rendering of speech in Hindi, while addressing tribal rally at Nandurbar, Pune, March 1989.

COMPARTMENTALIZATION OF INDIA

"It is the compartmentalization of India into rigidly separated rural and urban settlements that has been the worst legacy of the colonial system of local self-government."

Source: L.S. Deb, 7th August, 1989.

CONSTITUTIONALISATION OF GRASSROOTS DEMOCRACY

"The single greatest event in the evolution of democracy in India was the enactment of the Constitution which established democracy in Parliament and the State Legislatures. This historic revolutionary Bill takes its place alongside that great event as the enshrinement in the Constitution of democracy at the grassroots."

Source: C.K. Jain, "Rajiv Gandhi – His Role as a Constitutional Reformer" in *Rajiv Gandhi and Parliament* (ed.) C.K. Jain, New Delhi: CBS Publishers and Distributors, 1992, p. 185.

CONTAINING COMMUNALISM

"But the Forces of communalism have not accepted defeat. They are always on the prowl, always looking for an opportunity to make mischief, always trying to insinuate themselves into the political life of the country, working from behind the scenes or using others as a front. If the secular forces stand together communalism can be contained. The danger arises when political parties, for opportunistic reasons, lend the weight of their support of narrow causes."

Source: Intervention during a special discussion in the Lok Sabha on the communal situation, 3rd May, 1989.

COOPERATIVES FOR THE POOR

"The co-operative movement is a part of our freedom movement. The freedom struggle was waged not for political Independence only. It was waged with a view to bring India into the modern age and to enable our poor people, our backward people, to become stronger and able to compete with the rest of the world."

Source: Free rendering of speech in Hindi at the Indian Cooperative Maha Sammelan, New Delhi, 20th January, 1989.

COUNTRY WE WANT TO BUILD

"We have to build a country that Gandhiji and Panditji dreamed of, that Indiraji set out to build, where there is communal harmony, where we live as brothers and sisters, where we can hold our heads high – country which makes us proud to be a member of the comity of nations. Secularism cannot be indifference to religion, like I said, it must be a positive direction as Gandhiji and Panditji had shown us."

Source: Inaugural speech at the National Symposium on "India's Struggle Against Communalism", New Delhi, 8th October, 1986.

CRITICAL MASS WILL DO CRITICAL FUNCTION

"We believe the presence of women in large numbers in the Panchayats will not only make the Panchayats more representative but will also make them more efficient, honest, disciplined and more responsible."

Source: L.S. Deb, 15th May, 1989.

DEFAULTING MIND

"I am also the only surviving son of an assassinated mother. It takes a peculiarly sick mentality to insinuate that I could betray the love and affection that she showered upon me by restoring to the bureaucracy a suspected accomplice in her assassination. What manners of men are these who make such accusations? Their low insinuations are not a reflection on me, or on our Government, but on them, their thought processes, on the functioning of their minds, on the murky depths at which they function."

Source : Mani Shankar Aiyar, "Rajiv Gandhi in Parliament" in *Rajiv Gandhi and Parliament* (ed.) C.K. Jain, New Delhi: CBS Publishers and Distributors, 1992, p. 129.

DEFECTIVE EDUCATIONAL SYSTEM

"Today, we find the education system in India with many deficiencies and defects. Perhaps, the biggest problem and the root of the problem is that it does not deal with the world as it is today. We have inherited a system which the British have by and large left us, a system which was tailored to produce clerks to work in the offices in those days."

Source: Convocation address at Visva-Bharati, Santiniketan, 6th December, 1985.

DEMOCRACY AND DEVELOPMENT

"Democracy without Panchayati Raj is a negation of Mahatma Gandhi's dreams. Development without Panchayati Raj is a negation of Jawaharlal Nehru's Vision:

"Real Change" said Panditji, "come, of course, from within the village, from the very people living in the village, and is not imposed from outside.""

Source: Speech at the Conference of Chief Ministers on Panchayati Raj, New Delhi, 5th May, 1989.

DIALECTICS OF SECULARISM

"Notwithstanding thousands of years of secularism, the forces of communalism have not been vanquished. The history of India is a kind of dialectic between the forces of secularism, tolerance and compassion *versus* the forces of communalism, fundamentalism and fanaticism. In the long run, secularism will always triumph. But the never-ceasing running battle with the opposing forces of communalism continues, which we must fight."

Source: Intervention during a special discussion in the Lok Sabha on the communal situation, 3rd May, 1989.

DIGNITY OF THE HOUSE

"The House is a forum of debate where sharp exchanges take place and arguments and counter arguments are put forward. It is a forum where government is taken to task. It is a place where the Government has to defend itself and clarify its stand. During the course of the debate, nobody is spared and it is not expected also. But by maintaining the prestige and dignity of the House, we can stress the force of argument and maintain the goodwill."

Source: Dhanik Lal Mandal, "Rajiv – A Great Soul Dedicated to the Nation" in *Rajiv Gandhi and Parliament* (ed.) C.K. Jain, New Delhi: CBS Publishers and Distributors, 1992, pp. 66-67.

DISCIPLINING

"Responsibilities start with discipline—discipline in educational institutions, discipline in every sphere of life, perhaps most of all in government. The most important aspect of discipline in government is financial discipline, because if we do not maintain financial discipline then nothing can work, there can be no success."

Source: Inaugural address at the Golden Jubilee Celebrations of the University of Kerala, Trivandrum, 28th December, 1987.

DISTRICT ADMINISTRATION NOT A REPRESENTATIVE

"At present, most district administrations are not representative because we have allowed democratically elected local bodies to wither away. Even where elected local bodies do exist, planning and development functions are, to a large extent, divorced from these institutions. A district administration that is not a democratic administration cannot be a representative administration. A major systemic increase in responsiveness will arise out of making district administration more representative."

Source: Inaugural Speeches at the Workshops of District Collectors and Magistrates on Responsive Administration, Jaipur, 30th April, 1988.

EARTH CITIZEN

"At every stage, the progress of civilization has been associated with the enlargement of the area of group loyalty. The logical culmination of this process will be reached when the entire planet is regarded as one, when each inhabitant of our planet regards the earth as one, when all those who inhabit the world consider themselves as belonging to one family, when each of us evolves into a true Earth Citizen."

Source: Speech while inaugurating the second conference in memory of Indira Gandhi on the 'Making of an Earth Citizen', New Delhi, 16th January, 1989.

EDUCATION FOR THINKING

"We have to make our younger generation to think. Unfortunately the educational system as it is today, stops anyone from thinking. You prevent people from asking questions. You drill in a set syllabus and you ask him to reproduce that during the examination. This is not good enough. The system must be such that young boys and girls are provoked into asking questions, are provoked into making the teacher explain things they do not understand, instead of just memorizing it. It will not only be good for the children, it will be good for the teachers, because they will have to answer questions. The system will develop, new ideas will come, not only within the educational system but right across."

Source: Inaugural Address to the Conference of Education Ministers of States and Union Territories, New Delhi, 29th August, 1985.

EDUCATION IN OUR DAILY LIFE

"Modern education is the inculcation of a scientific spirit, in other words, developing an interest in science, in scientific thinking, in scientific methods, not necessarily in fundamental research, but in our daily lives, in our daily thinking. It is the cultivation of a logical mind, it is the development of a process of argument and discussions, it is the removing of inconsistencies, and superstitions."

Source: Inaugural address at the Silver Jubilee Celebrations of the National Council of Educational Research and Training, New Delhi, 11th September, 1986.

EDUCATION IS A GREAT EQUALIZER

"Education must be a great equalizer in our society. It must be the tool to level the differences that our various social systems have created over the past thousands of years. Education has to be the key. We have made many laws but social change cannot be brought about by legislation. It has to be brought about in society itself and the starting point has to be at the root and this is education."

Source: Speech at the one hundred and fiftieth anniversary of the Madras Christian College, Madras, 16th December, 1985.

EDUCATION IS NATION BUILDING

"What is important in education? This we must be very clear about. We have to teach that we are one nation, we have to teach that there are some basic values that we stand for, there is a basic ideology behind the country, there are some basic truths that we are standing for. Gandhiji taught us that truth and non-violence are the two basic truths, that is what we build our nation on. We cannot afford to have States ignoring the basic ethos of the country. Schooling is not just sending people into a room with no teachers in it and giving them a degree at the end of it. Schooling is creating a generation which can build this nation, which can strengthen this nation, which can make this nation strong enough to stand up against any other nation."

Source: Reply to the debate on the President's Address in Rajya Sabha, 4th March, 1987.

EFFICIENT PUBLIC SECTOR

"Our policy is to strengthen the pubic sector. The total commitment to the public sector is at the top of our economy. We will ensure its leading role. There is no question of privatization. We want to see, at the same time, a better functioning public sector. It is not good enough just to have a massive public sector which is flabby and does not move. An efficient public sector must be created which helps development which helps the country more forward, which generates wealth for the country; not a public sector which absorbs our wealth. We look for better performance in the public sector. We look for much higher productivity, increased generation of resources for investment and expansion of the public sector. This thrust and this concentration on the public sector is so that we can become self-reliant."

Source: Intervention in Rajya Sabha on Finance Bill, 1987, 7th March, 1987.

END COMMUNAL FORCES

"We have to save the country from such people, because such people will destroy our India. It is not the Government's responsibility alone. Of course, the Government has the responsibility but a much greater responsibility rests with the 80 crore people to raise a voice all over the country to prevent such communal forces from becoming strong, to prevent them from coming up. The country must find the strength to finish off these communal forces."

Source: Free rendering of speech in Hindi while laying the foundation stone of Haj Manzil, New Delhi, 28th August, 1989.

ENTRY TO POLITICS

"… I had no love for politics. I treasured the privacy of my happy family life. My mother respected both these sentiments. Then my brother, Sanjay was killed in the prime of his life. It broke a mother's heart. It did not break a Prime Minister's will. Without even a day's break of grief, she carried on her noble task single-minded in fulfilling her pledge to her people.

There is a loneliness that only a bereaved mother can know… she called to me in her loneliness. I went to her side. At her instance, I left my love for flying at her instance I joined her as a political aide. From her I learnt my first political lessons. It was she who urged me to respond to the insistent demand from the constituency and the party to take my brother's place as Member of Parliament for Amethi. With her blessings I was made General Secretary of my party asking me to accept the challenge of stepping into her shoes.

In accepting the challenge I fulfilled a national duty and a filial duty, the duty of a son to a mother."

Source: L.S Deb, 10th April, 1989, c.448.

ENVIRONMENT AND DEVELOPMENT

"While we are on our way to development, we tend to move away from nature. It should not be so. We are trying to go back to nature. We are trying to bring children closer to nature. We have to ensure that in our bid to progress, we do not do any such thing as to pollute the environment."

Source: Speech while inaugurating an exhibition on environment, New Delhi, 14th November, 1985.

EXTENSION WORK BY MEN

"Extension programmes for rural development, for agricultural development, are invariably carried out by men. They don't understand the problems of women in the rural areas."

Source: Inaugural speech at the International Conference on Appropriate Agricultural Technologies for Farm Women, New Delhi, 30th November, 1988.

FARMERS OUR BACKBONE

"If farmers become weak the country loses self-reliance but if they are strong, freedom also becomes strong. If we do not maintain our progress in agriculture, poverty cannot be eliminated from India.

But our biggest poverty alleviation programme is to improve the living standard of our farmers.

The thrust of our poverty alleviation programmes is on the uplift of the farmers."

Source: Inaugural Speech at the 25th National Convention of the Bharat Krishak Samaj, Hyderabad, 15th February, 1988.

FIGHTING COMMUNALISM AND TERRORISM

"The fight against communal forces must be fought unitedly. We are heirs to Gandhiji's heritage of communal harmony; to Panditji's scientific outlook; and to Indiraji's struggle against the forces of destabilization—terrorists, separatists and communalists. We cannot fail them. Communalism must not be used as a political tool. If I may read a sentence from the secret Will of Babar to his son, Humayun: It is incumbent on thee to wipe all religious prejudices of the tablet of thy heart."

Source : Mani Shankar Aiyar, "Rajiv Gandhi in Parliament" in *Rajiv Gandhi and Parliament* (ed.) C.K. Jain, New Delhi: CBS Publishers and Distributors, 1992, p. 119.

FIRST MAN TO THINK THIS ISSUE

"Thinking of this University today, we are reminded of Mahatma Gandhi because if there was anyone who fought for the weak in India, the first one to raise his voice for the Scheduled Castes, that was Gandhiji. There were social workers before him but not any people who raised this matter in the political arena as he did."

Source: Free rendering of Speech in Hindi after laying the foundation stone of Dr. Ambedkar University, Lucknow, 14th April, 1989.

FREEDOM AND RESPONSIBILITY

"The freedom of India has meant the freedom of the Press. To be committed to India's democracy is to be committed to freedom of expression. Every right carries with it a responsibility. Every freedom carries with it an obligation."

Source: Free rendering of speech in Hindi while addressing Tribal Rally at Nandurban, Pune, 31st March, 1989.

FREE PEOPLE

"A free people are a people who choose their own representatives. A free people are a people who are governed by their will and ruled with their consent. A free people are a people who participate in decisions affecting their lives and their destinies."

Source: L.S. Deb, 15th May, 1989.

GANDHIJI'S DREAM

"Gandhiji taught us that if India has to develop, if the people of India were to be really free, then this freedom and development have to start from village level. Only then can we really claim that we are free, Gandhiji strove hard but certain capitalist forces did not let him succeed. His hands were tied and development at that time could not start from the village level."

Source: Independence Day Speech (Hindi) from Red Fort, 15th August, 1989.

GAP BETWEEN PEOPLE AND GOVERNMENT

"There is a second deleterious consequences of the vast chasm that separates the general body of the electorate from the small number of its elected representatives. This gap has been occupied by the power-brokers, the middlemen, the vested interests."

Source: L.S. Deb, 15th May, 1989.

GIVE POWER TO THE PEOPLE

"We trust the people. We have faith in the people. It is the people who must determine their own destinies and the destiny of the nation. To the people of India, let us ensure maximum democracy and maximum devolution. Let there be an end to the power-brokers. Let us give power to the people."

Source: L.S. Deb, 15th May, 1989.

GOALS OF EDUCATION

"Education ultimately is the development of the human being and that cannot be restricted only to the classroom. It is a much wider term and that is what we are trying to do."

Source: Speech at the Golden Jubilee Celebrations of Doon School, Dehra Dun, 3rd November, 1985.

GOOD MUST BE UNITED

"Very few people are willing to talk about principles. We must remember that when anti-national, secessionist and communal forces joined hands in an unprincipled manner, India was divided. We must remember how this happened. Today, all our energies must be geared up to defeat the designs of communal, divisive, anti-national, feudal and conservative forces because if they join together, it would mean the division of India. The people of India must remember that if they allow these forces to unite and grow strong, India will disintegrate, her freedom will be lost and India would again become a slave."

Source: Independence Day speech (Hindi) from Red Fort, 15th August, 1989.

GOOD NEIGHBOURS

"It falls upon our generation to safeguard our sovereignties not through the illusory pursuit of military strength but through the conscious pursuit of friendship between ourselves. It falls upon us to silence the guns that have given no peace and to seek the enduring solutions that only peaceful co-existence can ensure. It falls upon us to work together in the great struggle that lies ahead…We are summoned to greater tasks than assiduously aggravating the scars of history. In the larger global context, we must rise above the stoking of petty problems, unworthy of our larger destiny…It is a destiny we can achieve together, as friends and good neighbours."

Source: Speech at a banquet hosted by Prime Minister of Pakistan, in Islamabad, 16th July, 1989.

GRASSROOTS IGNORED IN REFORM

"Unfortunately, when the bureaucracy is consulted on basic issues, the consultation is invariably at the top, at the upper echelons, and not at the cutting edge of development or at the district administration level. However, no matter what earth-shattering decisions or direction we might give from the top, the implementation and delivery is at the district level. And that really is in your hands. The way that delivery takes place, the efficiency of that delivery is in your hands. While a lot of attention has been paid at the higher level to reforms and other changes, the lower level, where the delivery to take place, has generally been neglected or ignored."

Source: Inaugural address at the workshop on Responsive Administration, Bhopal, 10th December, 1987.

HUMAN RESOURCE DEVELOPMENT

"We have recently clubbed together certain Ministries and labelled them "Human Resources Development" not because we wanted to give a fancy paint job but because what we really want is to develop the human resources. Today from every corner people tell 'population' what is happening! What is happening? Yes, it is one of our biggest problems. What we must do is to turn this problem into the biggest asset and that will happen if we are able to develop the human resources in our country and this is what we must attempt to do; develop them not just in teaching them technology, teaching them sciences or medicine or whatever... but also develop a sense of value and idealism, a commitment to the country, develop the cultural heritage that we have inherited. All this must be blended into one package."

Source: L.S. Deb, 18th December, 1985, cc.320-321.

HUMAN UNITY

"...It is only when we start seeing the world as one humanity that the strength of countries such as India, which rely on basic principles and values as opposed to brute force and alignment, it is then that our strength will come out. It is then that the world will become a truly livable place...If we fight against wrong attitude anywhere in the world it is because we want to change this attitude from one of "us" and "them" to "all of us" together, as one humanity."

Source: L.S. Deb, 3rd March, 1987, cc. 282-83.

I HAVE A DREAM

"India is an old country but a young nation: and like the young everywhere, we are impatient. I am young, and I too have a dream. I dream of an India—strong, independent, self-reliant and in the front rank of the nations of the world in the service of mankind. I am committed to realizing that dream through dedication, hard work and collective determination of our people."

Source : K.N. Singh, "Rajiv Gandhi – An Apostle of Peace" in *Rajiv Gandhi and Parliament* (ed.) C.K. Jain, New Delhi: CBS Publishers and Distributors, 1992, p. 158.

IDEA COMES THROUGH A PROCESS

"We have come to this House at the culmination of a process of open, transparent consultation without precedent in the history of independent India. The Amendments we present are the distilled essence of the views of thousands of elected local body representatives, hundreds of District magistrates, scores of senior government servants, and dozens of Ministers and Chief Ministers."

Source : Mani Shankar Aiyar, "Rajiv Gandhi in Parliament" in *Rajiv Gandhi and Parliament* (ed.) C.K. Jain, New Delhi: CBS Publishers and Distributors, 1992, p. 134.

IMPLICATIONS OF MASS MOVEMENTS

"It was out of this heightened social consciousness and commitment to social reform that the Independence Movement arose. That is why objectives of the movement were never limited to political independence.

Our freedom of this movement always saw freedom as the opportunity for social emancipation and economic progress. As the struggle for independence gathered force."

Source: Speech delivered at the Valedictory function of the Centenary Celebrations of *Malayala Manorama*, New Delhi, 18th March, 1989.

IMPORTANCE OF DIALOGUE

"There must be full discussion, because without debate there can be neither democracy nor a correct choice of path by us. Debate there must be, but it must be such that we follow our principles, our main tenets, and from that standpoint we examine what kind of programmes we are implementing and how we are progressing on the chosen path. Many times we see that there is less light and more heat in the way debates are conducted in our assemblies. So often we find some people arguing even with the Chair. Work does not proceed with indiscipline. This does not rebound to the credit of our democracy, not to the honour of our country. We must think seriously about how to run our Assemblies, whether noise and agitation bring honour to the nation, or whether we can progress by engaging in serious discussions on material points. It is so easy to get one's name into the newspapers of our regions, to make the headlines. It is a painful reflection that people tend to forget the great difficulties with which this freedom was attained, how much people had to struggle. If we make a joke of this freedom and throw it out of the window, there will be no saviour. Here, in such Assemblies, we have to establish that we are seriously prepared to defend that freedom, that today we are determined to struggle for the maintenance of the independence. In all seriousness, we have to show that Indian democracy is an example for the world. We have to look, not only at other developing nations, but also countries where democracy is long established, where it is a running concern and show them that our democracy is better, stronger, than theirs."

Source: Speech on the Occasion of the Golden Jubilee Celebrations of UP Vidhan Sabha, Lucknow, 19th December, 1987.

IMPORTANCE OF TRADITIONAL VALUES

"One of the most important aspects of the education system is the value system that it builds in our society. Unfortunately, for whatever reason, our society has drifted away from our traditional values."

Source: L.S. Deb, 3rd March, 1987.

IMPROVING EDUCATION

"Every educational system like any other system needs regular upkeep, maintenance, upgradation and improvements. No system can be the same for ever. It has to adjust with times, with development, with new discoveries in technologies."

Source: Inaugural Speech at the Seminar on "Implementation Strategies of the National Policy on Education", New Delhi, 26th June, 1986.

INDIA AND CHINA RELATIONS

"Our relation is crucial to the future of humankind. India and China seek an improvement in their relationship not only for their mutual benefits but also to provide the basis on which we can contribute to the building of a new world order."

Source: Speech at the State banquet hosted by the Chinese Premier Li Peng in Beijing, 19th December, 1988.

INDIA DEMONSTRATED

"Most civilizations posit nationhood and diversity as antithetical. The single greatest contribution of India to world civilization is to demonstrate that there is nothing antithetical between diversity and nationhood. Through 5000 years of living experience, we have demonstrated to the world that our unity in diversity is a vibrant reality."

Source: Intervention during a special discussion in the Lok Sabha on the communal situation, 3rd May, 1989.

INDIA HAD A TRADITION OF PANCHAYATS

"The tradition of Panchayats as institutions of local self-government is integral to the Indian tradition. It evolved in rural India where, till very recently, almost whole of India lived."

Source: Address at Conference of the Chief Ministers, New Delhi, 7th July, 1989.

INDIA IS IMMORTAL

"That is a moment of profound grief. The foremost need now is to maintain our balance. We can and must face this tragic ordeal with fortitude, courage and wisdom…India lives. India is immortal. The spirit of India is immortal…We shall shoulder the burden heroically and with determination….I shall value your guidance in upholding the unity, integrity and honour of the country."

Source: K.N. Singh, "Rajiv Gandhi – An Apostle of Peace" in *Rajiv Gandhi and Parliament* (ed.) C.K. Jain, New Delhi: CBS Publishers and Distributors, 1992, p. 159.

INDIA IS NOT ORDINARY NATION

"India is not just any other developing country. India's word, India's stand, India's position means something and this has come about with a solid work done by this government at every level."

Source: R.S. Deb, 2nd December, 1986.

INDIA IS SECOND TO NONE

"In the coming years, there should be no area, in which India is second to any other country in the world. In the past 37 years, we have developed an industrial infrastructure, we have developed a management cadre and we have developed tremendous technological know how. This is what we must use to take India into the next century, and not behind any other country, but equal to any other country in the world."

Source: Speech at Ferguson College, Pune, 1st June, 1985.

INDIA IS STRONG

"Today, people find a strong country forging steadily ahead with pride. Today, no one raise the question disintegration of the country because India has proved to the world that it is a power which cannot be weakened by anyone."

Source: Free rendering of the address in Hindi from the ramparts of the Red Fort on the occasion of Independence Day, New Delhi, 15th August, 1988.

INDIAN APPROACH TO INDIAN PROBLEM

"What we need is an Indian approach to Indian problems. We should not be looking for a Japanese or an American or a German solution to Indian problems."

Source: Inaugural address to the All India Businessmen's Convention, New Delhi, 12th March, 1986.

INDIAN UNITY IS STRENGTH

"If India is strong every Indian is strong; if India is weak every Indian will be weak. Our endeavour has always been to make the people of India strong and the future of the country secure. In our strength lies our honour, our progress. Being an Indian does not mean that we are mere inhabitants of this country. It means that we are inheritors of a splendid civilization of over five thousand years. We have a diversity of cultures. We belong to different religions – Hindus, Muslims, Sikhs, Christians, Jains, Parsis and Buddhists. We speak a variety of languages. Our tolerance makes all of them flourish. We accord equal respect to all faiths and religions. Our strength and unity flow from this fact. This is the only path we must follow, for our strength lies in our diversity."

Source: Free rendering of Independence Day speech in *Hindu* from the ramparts of the Red Fort, 15th August, 1986.

INDIAN WOMEN

"One of the biggest challenges we are facing in India today is to see how Indian women can be made self-reliant and brought into the mainstream of the nation-building process; how they can be made economically stronger; how they can be helped in developing. The attitude of suppressing or keeping women down are very deeply ingrained in our society and go back to many thousands of years."

Source: Speech while inaugurating a Science and Technology Institute after visiting the Adiparasakthi Temple, Meelmaruvathur, Tamil Nadu, 12th November, 1988.

INDIA'S HERITAGE

"India has a tremendously rich heritage of spirituality and not getting drawn into a materialistic attitude. This perhaps can be our biggest contribution to today's world and the future generation. Our civilization and heritage do not draw from anyone religion or from anyone saint or prophet. The strength of our culture and our heritage is that it has always synthesised, assimilated, absorbed what has been best anywhere in the world. It has also not hesitated to remove what is wrong in our own system. We have self-confidence for introspection and for correction."

Source: Speech while inaugurating a Science and Technology Institute after visiting the Adiparasakthi Temple, Meelmaruvathur, Tamil Nadu, 12th November. 1988.

INDIA'S NATIONALISM

"The essence of our present days nationalism lies in the greatness of our ancient culture. In order to exist as a nation, we will have to preserve our cultural identity. For this, we should give equal respect to the various aspects of our national life. Therefore, secularism is the corner stone of our existence as a nation. People of various religions, various languages and of various dialects have made India their home. In fact, cultural plurality is what India stands for. Each one of these diverse characteristics is important in its own way. Their identity is inseparable from that of India's identity, rather it is this plurality, this composite culture, which forms the basis of our identity as a nation, and in return, each one of these parts maintains its uniqueness as part and parcel of the great Indian nation."

Original in Hindi

Source: Dhanik Lal Mandal, "Rajiv – A Great Soul Dedicated to the Nation" in *Rajiv Gandhi and Parliament* (ed.) C.K. Jain, New Delhi: CBS Publishers and Distributors, 1992, pp. 63-64.

INDIA'S PLURALISM

"In modern day world, perhaps India's is the first experiment in the form of the pluralistic society. You look at any other country. I do not think that any other country has accepted such a challenge. Therefore, it is not just a challenge before us alone, rather it is an example for the whole world that despite all diversities, humanity as a whole can live as a family without any parochial barriers or schism. It is an ideal before the world that the values enshrined in our ancient philosophy depict the best way of life for India and the world as a whole."

Source: Dhanik Lal Mandal, "Rajiv – A Great Soul Dedicated to the Nation" in *Rajiv Gandhi and Parliament* (ed.) C.K. Jain, New Delhi: CBS Publishers and Distributors, 1992, pp. 64-65.

INDIA'S PROGRESS IS FELT

"During any period of change, during any time when a nation becomes much stronger, when it makes its presence felt in a bigger way, there are pressures. India is experiencing such pressures today."

Source: Speech while addressing the Golden Jubilee Celebrations of the *Assam Tribune*, New Delhi, 18th September, 1989.

INDIGENOUS BASE OF SCIENCE AND TECHNOLOGY

"With the Vision of Jawaharlal Nehru and Indira Gandhi, India has built a strong indigenous base of Science and Technology. This we have to put to good use in the coming years to enhance production in all sectors and make the economy dynamic and capable of holding on its own in the international arena. To this end we shall set up technology missions in key areas. We shall concentrate effort in frontier areas of science and technology to put ourselves abreast of advanced nations."

Source: Najma Heptulla, "Rajiv Gandhi As I Know Him", in *Rajiv Gandhi and Parliament* (ed.) C.K. Jain, New Delhi: CBS Publishers and Distributors, 1991, p. 82.

JAPAN'S UNIQUENESS

"We have much to learn from Japan—the technologies you have mastered, your methods of organizing production, the science of human relation in industry, and above all, the art of blending modern industrialization with ancient values."

Source: Address to Economic Organisations in Tokyo, 29th November, 1985.

LIFE LONG EDUCATION

"Education is not something which can be limited to educational institutions. It is not something that ends when you leave school or college. It must continue throughout life."

Source: L.S. Deb, 3rd March, 1987.

LINKAGE BETWEEN POVERTY AND TECHNOLOGY

"The poverty gap is essentially a technology gap. What separates the developed from the developing is the level of technology that is used directly or indirectly in the everyday life of our people. Within a country, what defines and distinguishes the better-off from the worse-off is, again the quantity and quality of technology that they use in their daily lives."

Source: Address at the Foundation laying function of the Indian National Academy of Engineering, New Delhi, 11th April, 1988.

LINKING TECHNOLOGY WITH FARMERS

"But the biggest question is how to inform the farmers about new techniques and developments taking place in other parts of the country and the world and the potentialities that these offer for them."

Source: Speech while inaugurating the National Agriculture Fair, New Delhi, 25th March, 1989.

LOCAL BODY IS PEOPLE'S RIGHTS

"Far from encroaching on States' rights, we have displayed the utmost sensitivity to the structure of Centre-State relationships built through the Constitution. Entry Five of the State List remains untouched. The sovereignty of State Legislatures remains undiminished. We are amending the Constitution, not drafting municipal law on a State subject. What is being taken away is the right to ignore the people. What is being removed is the right to flout the people's will. What is being ended is the reign of the power-brokers. It is not a question of the Centre's rights *versus* the States' rights. It is a question of the people's rights."

Source: Statement in the Lok Sabha while introducing the Constitution (65th Amendment) Bill, 7th August, 1989.

MAINSTREAMING WOMEN

"There is no section of our society more oppressed, more exploited and more neglected than women. In every segment, class or community, women suffer all the disabilities inflicted on that group and, in addition, suffer also the consequences of gender discrimination. Yet, their contribution to economic life, social well-being, cultural continuity and ethical standards is far great than their share of the population. We must make a determined beginning to bring women into the mainstream of local self-government."

Source: Statement in the Lok Sabha while introducing the Constitution (65th Amendment) Bill, 7th August, 1989.

MAKE INDIA A MODEL

"We have the opportunity before us to give India a new personality in the world. Today we have an opportunity to make India as great as she was before her slavery. Before India lost her freedom, people from different corners of the world came to India to discover her wealth and to acquire knowledge. But hundreds of years of slavery have emaciated India. India degenerated and became poor and weak. Today for the first time, we have an opportunity to restore India to the same old glorious position. We have to remove poverty and injustice from India. We have to make India self-reliant. We have to develop India into a great power in the world but not like other great powers who have risen by suppressing others."

Source: Independence Day Speech (Hindi) from Red Fort, 15th August, 1989.

MAKE POWER BROKERS OUT

"In driving the power-brokers out of the power-houses, in rendering the panchayats to the people, we lay upon the people's representatives the solemn responsibility of turning their attention, first and foremost, to the needs of the poorest, the more deprived and the most in need."

Source: L.S. Deb, 15th May, 1989.

MAN WITH MODERN TECHNOLOGY

"Man with modern technology at his command has for the first time the power to destroy the environment around him and create a situation from which he will not be able to come out, no matter how technology advanced may be."

Source: Manmohan Singh, "Rajiv Gandhi — A Visionary" in *Rajiv Gandhi and Parliament* (ed.) C.K. Jain, New Delhi: CBS Publishers and Distributors, 1992, p. 62.

MANDATE FOR UNITY AND STRENGTH

"Administrative reform is crucial for social and economic transformation. It is for this reason that I decided to take under my own charge the Department of Personnel and Administrative Reforms. A full-scale review of administrative organization, policies and procedures is in progress.

I have asked that the decision-making processes should be decentralized along with enforcement of accountability. Rule and procedures will be drastically simplified to speed up decision-making. Results will take precedence over procedures.

I have directed all concerned agencies to ensure that citizens get prompt and courteous service from Government departments and agencies. An effective machinery for redressal of public grievances will be set up in offices and departments with large public dealings.

Action will be taken to raise the morale of public services. We shall prevent extraneous interference in the normal functioning of public services. We must create a new administrative culture for service of the masses."

Source: Broadcast to the nation, 5th January, 1985.

MASS EDUCATION

"What is needed, therefore, is a very massive education process for the people, so they understand and then they demand what they really need for their development, for economic development."

Source: Speech at the Valedictory session of National Convention Against Communal and Divisive Forces, New Delhi, 6th October, 1988.

MIND AND MATTER

"There are three basic questions that we must face today. The first, perhaps, must be the question of the motivation for growth, for development. The second which we in India are already faced with is that of a westernization, a materialism, a consumerism. The third, perhaps, the most important is the question of how we relate scientific and technological development to the more philosophical, the more human side of development, and how we are to narrow the gap between these two streams of development."

Source: Address to the special session of the Indian Philosophical Congress, Hyderabad, 19th December, 1985.

MISSING CONCERN FOR ENVIRONMENT

"Since the beginning of creation, man has lived in harmony together with nature and in atmosphere of mutual respect, mutual dependence except in recent centuries, since the Industrial Revolution, when man has alienated himself from nature, when man has not realized the potential of damage that he has unleashed on nature. During this period we have discovered the very heavy cost of ignoring environment and looking at development as a purely very short-sighted economic exercise, as opposed to a wider perspective encompassing the environment and the larger effects that it has on everything."

Source: Valedictory address at the Seminar on Ecological and Conservation Research, New Delhi, 13th April, 1987.

MODERNITY AND TRADITION

"We want tribal cultures to be preserved even while the Adivasis march ahead on the path of development. And this is not easy. Because when we start working, readymade development patterns are immediately adopted and generally these are different from the work-culture and traditional patterns of the Adivasis. That is why Panditji offered them special protection, gave them special safeguards. Reservations were provided and steps to protect the Adivasis in every way written into the Constitution."

Source: Free rendering of speech in Hindi while addressing Tribal Rally at Nandurban, Pune, 31st March, 1989.

NEED OF CHANGE IN EDUCATIONAL SYSTEM

"The educational system also needs very substantial revision. The educational system has to be such that there is a basic national syllabus which builds an integrated India. The educational system has to be strengthened to bind our country together. It cannot be left to certain parties to take the educational system totally at a tangent. We will not allow this to happen."

Source: R.S. Deb, 23rd January, 1985.

NEED OF OPPOSITION

"…I want a good Opposition. That's what is worrying me…I want an Opposition which can stand across the floor and argue about politics, which can argue about future of the nation. An Opposition which is tied up in personal problems cannot help the nation…I have said so publicly; I have said so in public meetings; I have said so in Press conferences—that I would welcome a strong Opposition. I would welcome an Opposition that stands on principles and values…."

Source: L.S. Deb, 11th December, 1987, c. 449.

NEED OF REFORM IN ADMINISTRATION

"Administrative reform is crucial for social and economic transformation. It is for this reason that I decided to take under my own charge the Department of Personnel and Administrative Reforms. A full-scale review of administrative organization, police and procedures is in progress.

I have asked that the decision-making processes should be decentralized along with enforcement of accountability. Rules and procedures will be drastically simplified to speed up decision-making. Results will take precedence over procedures.

I have directed all concerned agencies to ensure that citizens get prompt and courteous service from Government departments and agencies. An effective machinery for redressal of public grievances will be set up in offices and departments with large public dealings.

Action will be taken to raise the morale of public services. We shall prevent extraneous interference in the normal functioning of public services. We must create a new administrative culture for service of the masses."

Source: Broadcast to the Nation, 5th January, 1985.

NEED OF REFORM IN EDUCATION

"Our educational system needs to be reconstructed as a dynamic force for national growth and integration. I intend to initiate a comprehensive review of the system and to build a national consensus for reform."

Source: Broadcast to the nation, 12th November, 1984.

NEHRU STOOD FOR DEMOCRACY

"We remember Jawaharlal Nehru, the maker of modern India. It was he who breathed democracy into the life of the nation. It was he who inscribed secularism in our hearts. He gave us planning and socialism. He elaborated the philosophy and policies of non-alignment. It was Jawaharlal Nehru who reminded us that our labours are not for ourselves alone but for all humankinds."

Source: Speech at the commemorative session of Parliament to mark the 40th Anniversary of Independence, New Delhi, 13th August, 1987.

NEW THEORY IN DEMOCRACY

"My second proposition is that democracy is in no way incompatible with economic development. Perhaps, growth has sometimes been faster under a different system. But our own experience is that breakdowns are fewer, course correction faster and discontinuity avoided when there is debate and dissent than when there is unquestioning conformity."

Source: Jodidi Lecture at Harward University, 18th October, 1987.

NEW THEORY OF INDIAN DEMOCRACY

"My first proposition is that lack of literacy does not come in the way of genuine democracy. India's experience amply demonstrates that illiteracy does not handicap the voter in knowing where his interest lies. The voter recognizes that there is a choice. And that the choice is a meaningful one. He exercises his options with an informed awareness of the issues. This political consciousness derives from the experience of generations who were swept in the independence struggle. It is reinforced by a free Press, the largest in the world, aggressive, investigative, and unfettered. It is wisdom that matters, not literacy."

Source: Jodidi Lecture at Harvard University, 18th October, 1987.

NOT PEOPLE'S FAULT

"It is by no means the people's fault that this sense of responsibility for their own well-being, progress and growth has not percolated to the grassroots. The fault lies with us in that neither democracy nor the devolution of power nor the assignment of responsibilities has been assured or effectively undertaken at the cutting-edge where the people and the administration meet."

Source: Address at a Conference of Chief Ministers, New Delhi, 7th July, 1989.

OBJECTIVES OF EDUCATION

"The objectives of education basically are freedom of the individual, a fulfilment in his life, equality among all our people, excellence of each individual, individual and collective self-reliance, and perhaps most of all, national cohesion."

Source: Inaugural Address at the 39th Meeting of the National Development Council on Education Policy, New Delhi, 29th April, 1986.

OUR ADMINISTRATIVE MALADIES

"In many ways, our present system is not the most dynamic when it comes to looking at solving problems. We pick the brightest brains in the nation. We train them for a year, perhaps two years, and then we sort of throw them into the wide ocean and for the next 30 or 35 years, we leave them to sink to swim on their own. We don't give you an adequate indication of the direction in which to swim. Every now and then, we have a sort of ad hoc evaluation of whether you are swimming well enough, fast enough, or whether you are swimming in the right direction. If we find that you are not, then we clobber you on the head. And of course, clobbering doesn't help you swim any better or faster. It only help you sink. Now we would like to change that. We would like to improve your swimming, give you direction and, perhaps, increase your speed."

Source: Inaugural speeches at the Workshops of District Collectors and Magistrates on Responsive Administration, Hyderabad, 13th February, 1988.

OUR ADMINISTRATIVE SYSTEM

"Our administrative system must become more goal-oriented. A new work-ethic, a new work-culture must be evolved in which Government is result-bound and not procedure-bound. Reward and punishment must be related to performance. A strong concern for efficiency must permeate all institutions."

Source: Broadcast to the Nation, 12th November, 1984.

OUR EXPERIENCE IN GRASSROOTS DEMOCRACY

"The experience of thirty years of democracy and development at the grassroots has varied enormously from State to State. There is no State where the experiment has not been tried, either through Panchayati Raj Institutions or through traditional bodies. Equally, there is no State which can claim to have reached perfection in running the institutions of Panchayati Raj. Yet, there has been little cross-fertilization or interaction between the Panchayati Raj systems of different States."

Source: Speech at the Conference of Chief Ministers on Panchayati Raj, New Delhi, 5th May, 1989.

OUR POLITICS

"We are not a people to shy away from our imperfections. On the contrary, we tend to exaggerate them. In western democracies, your articulate middle-class your more vocal segments are not consumed by politics. In India, politics is close to being an obsession. Some of us live politics and those who do not live politics, talk and breathe politics, we make instant judgement and would consider ourselves less than evolved if we did not have a snap opinion to offer on every issue."

Source: Jodidi Lecture at Harvard University, 18th October, 1987.

OUR SCIENCE AND TECHNOLOGY

"Unless we are able to give science and technology in India, not just imported science and technology, but Indian science and technology a major thrust. We will not be able to keep up this self-sufficiency that we have generated so far."

Source: R.S. Deb, 17th December, 1985.

OUR SYSTEM OF DEMOCRACY

"Our greatest asset is the system given to us by our forefathers. We have seen that the system is in tune with our ancient traditions and our culture, which have flourished uninterrupted for thousands of years. We used that spirit in our struggle for freedom and should use it in building a new India. Today, our greatest attainment is our democracy."

Source: Free rendering of speech in Hindi from the ramparts of the Red Fort on the occasion of the Independence Day, New Delhi, 15th August, 1987.

OUR WEALTH

"Our greatest wealth is our people. We must enable individuals and families to realize their potential to the full. For this we shall stress programmes of family planning, nutrition, welfare of women and children, control of disease, elementary and adult education sports and better communications."

Source: Broadcast to the Nation, 12th November, 1984.

PANCHAYATS AND SOCIAL JUSTICE

"We wanted to remove social injustice and atrocities on the weaker sections but this task has not yet been completed. Even today atrocities are perpetrated on weaker sections, on Scheduled Castes and Scheduled Tribes and on women. We want to involve people in nation building. We want everyone in the country to take initiative in such work. This, however, has not been fully accomplished and the result is that a system of power-brokers has emerged in our country, whether it is politics or the development process. For any work that is to be done, people have to please some power-broker. We have to break this system and to do this, we have to devolve maximum power to Panchayati Raj Institutions."

Source: Free rendering of speech in Hindi while inaugurating the Panchayati Raj Sammelan of Northern States, New Delhi, 27th January, 1989.

PANCHAYATS ON THEIR OWN FEET

"If the panchayats have to depend on the money provided by the State administration or the district administration, they can never gain any strength. If the panchayats do not stand on their own feet they can never make progress. And the panchayats will be able to stand on their own feet when they show the political will to find resources in the villages they cover. This is not to say that they must entirely depend on local resources, but so long as there is no involvement of the people, so long as there is no political will to organize local resources, the panchayats cannot become strong."

Source: Inaugural address to the 13th All India Panchayat Parishad, New Delhi, 22nd September, 1986.

PANDITJI AND PANCHAYATI RAJ

"Panditji very much wanted to fulfil Gandhiji's dream of Gram Swaraj. To achieve this, he started Panchayati Raj. But he could not complete the task. He could not accomplish this mission because of the infiltration of power-brokers who did not allow it to succeed. They ensured that real power did not slip out of their hands into the hands of the people of Bharat. After introducing Panchayati Raj Bill, Panditji did not live long to fight the power-brokers to ensure that the power that Gandhiji had wrested from the British reached the people."

Source: Independence Day Speech (Hindi) from Red Fort, 15th August, 1989.

PARTICIPATORY GROWTH AND DEMOCRACY

"Also, democracy cannot long survive paternalistic models of economic growth. A vibrant democracy demands participatory growth. We are making decisions regarding what is good for the people at all levels far removed from the people. We are then implementing these plans through the machinery that is alien to the people's will. This has led to a peculiar psychological and sociological syndrome in which the people believe that they have a right to development but not a responsibility for development. The assertion of a right without a recognition of the corresponding responsibility translates into unreal expectations, unrelated to real constraints of resources, unrelated to the inescapable need to make choices between alternative uses, unrelated to the imperative of raising resources, deploying them intelligently among competing needs, and phasing the fulfilment of expectations according to sensibly perceived priorities."

Source: Address at a Conference of Chief Ministers, New Delhi, 7th July, 1989.

PATRIOTISM

"Let us make no mistake: the challenges that the country faces are no ordinary challenges. There are forces in the world who want to see India falter and be mired in internal squabbles. There are forces that actively encourage terrorism. There are forces that aim to deflect us from our chosen path. These forces must be met squarely. The only way to do so is to place national interest above the interest of group, class or party. That is what patriotism means. Patriotism may be a somewhat old-fashioned word, but let me assure you that it is a virtue that can never become outdated."

Source: Address at the Silver Jubilee function of *Patriot*, New Delhi, 29th March, 1988.

PEN HAS LOST ITS STRENGTH

"There was a time when our Press used to have serious discussion on ideologies. There was a time when they relied on the power of their pen.

Those lofty ideals, where have they gone now? Where have those principles of truth gone? Today the pen has lost its strength and we have taken to the streets. From ideologies we have stooped down to slogan-shouting. There is really a misfortune for our nation."

Source: Speech while inaugurating the Golden Jubilee Celebrations of the National Herald, New Delhi, 9th September, 1988.

PEOPLE ARE ALWAYS SECULAR

"By and large, our people have reminded profoundly secular. Their deep religiosity only fosters an abiding respect for all faiths. Yet, fundamentalists and fanatics, revivalists and reactionaries do succeed, from time to time, in stoking the embers of communal violence."

Source: Address at the lunch hosted by the Foreign Policy Association, Asia Society and the India Chamber of Commerce, New York, 19th October, 1987.

PEOPLE IS OUR WEALTH

"Our greatest wealth is our people. We must enable individuals and families to realize their potential to the full. For this we shall stress programmes of family planning, nutrition, welfare of women and children, control of disease, elementary and adult education, sports and better communications."

Source: Broadcast to the nation, 12th November, 1984.

PEOPLE'S FAITH IN OUR DEMOCRACY

"Our people have casted their votes in very large numbers. There are very few countries of the world where such a heavy turn out of voters can be seen. There are very few countries of the world whose population pays such attention to the finer points of politics as does ours; every matter is debated and discussed at the tea shops. This is characteristic of our democracy and its real strength. That is what builds up the strength of the Assemblies. This strength has given strength to India."

Source: Free rendering of speech in Hindi on the occasion of the Golden Jubilee Celebrations of U.P. Vidhan Sabha, Lucknow, 19th December, 1987.

PERCEPTION ON BUREAUCRACY

"I want result-oriented bureaucracy not a procedure-oriented bureaucracy. A bureaucracy must achieve results or face the axe."

Source: Group Captain Ranbir Singh & M. Khosla, *Rajiv Gandhi: The Man, the Pilot, the Politician*, 1992, p. 45.

PERFECTION FOR PROFESSIONALISM

"We have to cultivate a positive work ethic, a work culture that gives us a productivity and quality in our goods whether they are finely crafted works of art or whether they are industrial goods. We have to get a certain standard of perfection. We have to have a feeling in a man who is making it, who is processing it, to try to strive for the very best, try for perfection and not to be satisfied with a half completed job. We have to invoke a certain social responsibility in our society. We have to see how we can adapt ourselves from what we are to what we would like to be and where we would like to take India."

Source: Speech at the inauguration of Eastern Zonal Centre for Culture, Santiniketan, 5th December, 1985.

PLAN WITHOUT PEOPLE'S PARTICIPATION

"There is a distancing of the people from the planning process. Increasingly the plan has become a technical document prepared by specialists, laying down a framework which planning experts might consider desirable, but to which the people and their representatives have made little contribution. It is a plan which hands down to the people targets set from above, with little or no consultation on what it is they want. It leaches their sense of responsibility for making their own contribution, and their own sacrifice, to the process of development.

The basic cause for this is that our democracy, firmly entrenched though it is in Parliament and State Assemblies, has been allowed to wither at the roots. Panchayati Raj Institutions have fallen into desuetude or drained of the effective role in the development process. All the more important agencies of planning, implementation and monitoring at the district and sub-district levels are dominated by the bureaucracy or by distant authorities from the State capitals. At the interface of the people and the development process, neither the people nor the local representatives have any effective say or involvement."

Source: Speech at the National Conference on Indian Planning Experience, New Delhi, 11th February, 1989.

PLANNING FROM BELOW

"We ensure that the voice of the people, their felt needs, their aspirations, their priorities become the building blocks of the edifice of planning. We must put an end to planning from above. We must put an end to priorities being conceived and decided at ethereal heights, far removed from the realities on the ground. We must put an end to paternalistic planning. We must initiate a process of people's planning."

Source: L.S. Deb, 15th May, 1989.

POVERTY REDUCTION

"All our pledges and all the measures we might take will be nullified if we fail to remove poverty in our country. So, we are focusing our special attention to poverty alleviation programmes. Wherever there are loopholes, we are trying to plug them and implement our programmes more vigorously. Where extra help is needed we are ready to give it. We are reviewing these programmes and will shortly bring forth a modified programme structured in a manner that will ensure greater benefits to the poor and lesser financial involvement of the administration."

Source: Free rendering of Independence Day speech in Hindi from the ramparts of Red Fort, 15th August, 1985.

POWER OF INDIAN YOUTH

"We have full faith in the youth of India. The youth of India have demonstrated their wisdom, their maturity in Panchayat elections, local body elections, and we feel that they are now ready to participate fully in the democratic process. This amendment will bring in almost 50 million people into the electoral system."

Source: C.K. Jain, "Rajiv Gandhi – His Role as a Constitutional Reformer" in *Rajiv Gandhi and Parliament* (ed.) C.K. Jain, New Delhi: CBS Publishers and Distributors, 1992, p. 183.

POWER TO PEOPLE

"It is essential to give power to the common people. We have to pay special attention to the weaker sections, the Scheduled Castes, the Scheduled Tribes and women. We have also to take special care of linguistic and other minorities and protect them. We have also to keep a watch so that devolution of power to grassroots is not usurped by the rich and those who derive power from the caste structure."

Source: Free rendering of speech in Hindi while inaugurating the Panchayati Raj Sammelan of Northern States, New Delhi, 27th January, 1989.

PROCESS OF NATIONAL INTEGRATION

"National Integration cannot be brought about just by putting it in the Constitution. If something that each one of us has to build into the social system of the country. It must come in through our democratic and secular system. It must come in through our economic policies and most of all through the political stances that we take, specially at times of elections or tensions.

We still find that communal incidents erupt in various parts of the country. We should get together on a policy, on a programme, to prevent all such incidents and attempts. This has to be a continuous battle which we will have to fight."

Source: Address to the first meeting of the reconstituted National Integration Council, New Delhi, 7th April, 1986.

PUBLIC AWARENESS

"Now, we have had reservations in this country for Scheduled Tribes and Scheduled Castes for over 35 years and you will be surprised to know that in one state, perhaps I shouldn't name that State where 55 per cent of the Scheduled Castes in urban areas did not know that reservations existed even after 35 years of Independence. So, it just shows that what we think we are doing, pretend we are doing, is not in fact happening because people don't even know what is available to them."

Source: Speech while inaugurating the International Symposium on Social Change Through Public Service Advertising, New Delhi, 10th August, 1989.

PUBLIC SECTOR

"The role of the public sector has to be better defined and perhaps the roles of different public sectors have to be defined differently. There will be certain public sector industries whose role should only be to give us good return, but that role cannot be stretched to all public sector industries. There is a social aspect to it, there is a strengthening-the-nation aspect to it. There is a much broader perspective in which we must look at the public sector."

Source: Intervention in Parliament on General Budget discussion and Demand for Excess Grants, 13th March, 1987.

QUALITY AND PEOPLE CENTRIC EDUCATION

"Our universities are a human resource base for centres of excellence. They are the agencies for translating research into action. We look to our New Education Policy to preserve, nurture and foster excellence. We are looking for a massive quality of upgradation in our schools and in our universities. We hope that this will lead to a massive increase in the qualitative levels of the scientific output from these institutions. The quality of Indian science must equal the quality of our educational institutions and our management. They must be involved in the creative process. There is too much red-tape, bureaucratic delays and tolerance of irrelevance and mediocrity which must be removed. The challenge is to make science not an esoteric pursuit, but relevant to the welfare and well-being of people everywhere."

Source: Address at the Valedictory session of the Indian Science Congress, Bangalore, 7th January, 1987.

RECAPTURE THE SPIRIT OF INDIA

"India is a very rich country, rich in spirituality, rich in an inner strength, in a depth which we don't find in other countries. Today, unfortunately, we only talk about material or economic benefit. This is not sufficient. For the proper nourishment of a human being much more is required than just mere economic betterment. And we must strive for this today."

Source: Speech after receiving the 1984 Dr. B.C. Roy National Award conferred posthumously on Shrimati Indira Gandhi, New Delhi, 30th April, 1985.

REFORM OUR ADMINISTRATIVE SYSTEM

"We need to look at the whole administrative system in the country, not just the IAS or the Revenue Service or any other service. We need to re-relate the system, each service in a particular manner according to our priorities. The priorities in hierarchy need not be priorities in emoluments and salaries. Certain technical areas will need to be looked at with special attention. We need to see that frustration does not develop in any service because they cannot rise above a particular point. This is a very big task."

Source: Inaugural address at the All India Income Tax Commissioners Conference, New Delhi, 4th June, 1987.

REFORMING ELECTIONS

"Let me say very clearly that his Bill is a major Bill. It is a major electoral reform. I would go to the extent of calling it historical and revolutionary and we have brought it in the Centenary Year of Panditji significantly. It will strengthen the roots of our democracy and it re-establishes the faith of the Congress in the youth of India and in the wisdom of the people of India."

Source: C.K. Jain, "Rajiv Gandhi – His Role as a Constitutional Reformer" in *Rajiv Gandhi and Parliament* (ed.) C.K. Jain, New Delhi: CBS Publishers and Distributors, 1992, p. 183.

RELIGION IS PERSONAL

"... is that religion has high value but must remain in the sphere of private and personal life. It has no role to play in the politics of the country."

Source: Intervention during a special discussion in the Lok Sabha on the communal situation, 3rd May, 1989.

REMEMBERING GANDHIJI

"Gandhiji gave us our heritage back. Gandhiji fought for change in our society, but all the time Gandhiji kept the poorer sections of our society at the forefront of his struggle. Gandhiji saw that unless every task that we do is aimed at the uplift of the poor, we cannot become stronger, we cannot win and preserve our Independence. It is this struggle to remove poverty, to uplift the poor which is our major challenge today. Every task that we do is aimed at the uplift of the poor, at removing poverty, at removing some of the suffering."

Source: Speech at Gandhi Jayanti Celebrations, Gandhigram, Tamil Nadu, 2nd October, 1988.

RESERVATION OF SEATS FOR SC/ST AND IMPERATIVE

"In my discussions with Panchayati Raj representatives, both during my extensive tours of rural India and in the numerous Panchayati Raj Sammelans we have held, it was brought home to me most forcefully that the democratic rights of the Scheduled Castes and the Scheduled Tribes cannot be secured by good intentions alone. At this stage, it has to be secured, in the first instance, by reservations in Panchayati Raj Institutions on the same basis as reservations are given in the Lok Sabha and the State Assemblies. I see that a certain section of the House is not happy about this. There is a widespread and justified apprehension on the part of the Scheduled Castes and the Scheduled Tribes that if their due representation in these bodies is not assured, Panchayati Raj could become an instrument of oppression in the hands of the rural elite."

Source: Statement while introducing the Constitution (64th Amendment) Bill on Panchayati Raj in Lok Sabha, 15th May, 1989.

RESPONSIVE ADMINISTRATION

"Our administration is also plagued with enormous wastage. The costs of administration eat up a disproportionately high share of the total outlay for schemes and programmes. Leakages of various other kinds occur. The people watch on helplessly as their representatives have little say, and no control, over what is happening. To the proposition that a responsive administration can only be a representative administration, I would add the other proposition that an efficient administration can only be a representative administration."

Source: Speech at the Conference of Chief Ministers on Panchayati Raj, New Delhi, 5th May, 1989.

ROLE OF CENTRE AND STATE IN STRENGTHENING PANCHAYATS

"... the Centre and the States share the responsibility for bringing Panchayati Raj to fruition. The Constitutional framework for Panchayati Raj is primarily the responsibility of the Centre. The legislative details fall in the province of the States. When we look back on thirty years of country-wide experience of Panchayati Raj, the picture that emerges is not one of the fulfilment of this Directive Principle of State Policy, but one of experiments, some more successful, some less, of experiments persisted with and experiments abandoned, of lessons learned and lessons unlearned, of a diversity of experience, some of which call for recognition and some for national transmission."

Source: Speech at the Conference of Chief Ministers on Panchayati Raj, New Delhi, 5th May, 1989.

ROLE OF POWER BROKERS

"For the minutest municipal function, the people have had to run around finding persons with the right connections who would intercede for them with the distant sources of power. The system has been captured by the power-brokers. It is being operated in the interests of the power-brokers. It is being protected by the power-brokers. The power-brokers have established their vice-like grip only because democracy has not functioned at the grassroots."

Source: L.S. Deb, 15th May, 1989.

ROLE OF PRESS IN COMBATING COMMUNALISM

"... Perhaps one of the most dangerous issues for a country like India is communalism. With the rise of certain communal forces, there is a danger of the sort that we have not had before. There is talk of a Hindu Rashtra, I don't see debate in our press on the consequences of Hindu Rashra. You have fought during the freedom struggle to keep Assam and North-East as part of India. I would like to ask the nation a question. If there is a Hindu Rashra, will the North-East become a Christian Rashra? Will it remain a part of India? What will happen in Punjab? Will it be a Sikh Rashtra? What will happen in Jammu and Kashmir? Will it become an Islami Rashra? These are very basic questions. Why are we fighting shy? Why is the press not picking up basic issues like these?"

Source: Speech while addressing the Golden Jubilee Celebrations of the *Assam Tribune*, New Delhi, 18th September, 1989.

ROOTS OF DEMOCRACY STRENGTHENED

"Let me say at the outset that the legislation that this Government has brought is a major legislation as it is aimed at strengthening the roots of our democracy. Our Indian democracy is unique in many ways. It is a unique experiment which is of global interest. It is the first time that a diverse society, with diverse cultures, with ethnically different people, speaking different languages, inhabiting different regions, professing different religions and having different castes, has been brought under one democratic system. In a sense, it is the microcosm of the world as also a demonstration to the world that democracy is possible amongst a diverse society such as ours which can be a model for an international democracy for people to live together on the globe."

Source: C.K. Jain, "Rajiv Gandhi – His Role as a Constitutional Reformer" in *Rajiv Gandhi and Parliament* (ed.) C.K. Jain, New Delhi: CBS Publishers and Distributors, 1992, pp. 182-83.

RURAL-URBAN CONTINUUM

"We have to get out of the colonial categorization of India into separate rural and urban boxes. We have to replace the compartmentalization of rural and urban India by a rural-urban continuum, which threads the farthest rural hamlet to the largest megapolis in a *rudrakshamala* of democracy and devolution."

Source: Statement in the Lok Sabha while introducing the Constitution (65th Amendment) Bill, 7th August, 1989.

SAFEGUARDING OUR FREEDOM

"Our leaders got us freedom and entrusted us with the responsibility of safeguarding and maintaining that freedom. It is our responsibility to protect it."

Source: Free rendering of speech in Hindi from the ramparts of the Red Fort on the occasion of the Independence Day, New Delhi, 15th August, 1987.

SCIENCE AND ENVIRONMENT

"If science is essential to development, it is indispensable for sustained development. The environmental imperative has now, fortunately, made its mark on the development scene. In many ways, the origins of the recognition of the interface between the environment and development can be traced back to Indiraji's Keynote Address at the Stockholm Conference on the environment held in 1972. The Report presented to the United Nations by Prime Minister Gro Harlem Brundtland has focused world attention on these issues. There is a national and an international dimensions to these issues."

Source: Address at the Indian Science Congress, Madurai, 7th January, 1989.

SCIENCE FOR EVERYDAY LIFE

"Science and technology is sometimes, especially in India, seen as something very sophisticated which is meant only for a few people to use. That is not so. Science and technology that is sophisticated and only for the very few, is really for the laboratories. When we talk of science and technology, we talk of the application of that in our everyday lives, in methods which become so mundane that we do not even realise the type of technology we are using when we are doing something."

Source: Inaugural address at the "Science and Village Exhibition", New Delhi, 14th November, 1987.

SCIENTIFIC TEMPER

"Once we have a scientific temper, basically it will remove the fear of the unknown which keeps people back, which keeps people from moving ahead and using the tools that are available to them. The scientific temper will help develop an inquisitive spirit...It is only when we start thinking...that a scientific temper will develop and we ourselves will start improving the tools that we have got and that we live with."

Source: L.S. Deb, 10th April, 1986, c.408.

SCIENTIFIC TEMPER

"The scientific temper can be looked at in two aspects. First, ordered thought, logical thinking, going from an established fact to the provable conclusion, subject to intuitive insight, rigorous inductive deduction, the testing of intellectual integrity, the readiness to relinquish a view when proved untenable, however, long-held and well-favoured. The second aspect is equally important: a questioning, probing, restless mind which takes nothing for granted, challenges any assumption and any convention, a mind that refuses to acquiesce in anything shoddy, that demands the best, that insists on bettering even the best."

Source: Address at the valedictory session of the India Science Congress, Bangalore, 7th January, 1987.

"As secular India alone is an India that can survive. Perhaps an India that is not secular does not deserve to survive... We are a multi-religious society, we are a multi-lingual society, we are a multi-cultural society, but we are not a multi-national society. We are one people, we are one country and we have one common citizenship... Most civilizations posit nationhood and diversity as antithetical. The single greatest contribution of India to world civilization is to demonstrate that there is nothing antithetical between diversity and nationhood. Through 5000 years of living experience, we have demonstrated to the world that our unity in diversity is a vibrant reality... Notwithstanding thousands of years of secularism, the forces of communalism have not been vanquished. The history of India is a kind of dialectic between the forces of secularism, tolerance and compassion *versus* the forces of communalism, fundamentalism and fanaticism. In the long run, secularism will always triumph but the never ceasing running battle with the opposing forces of communalism continues... How do we understand secularism? First and foremost, our secularism is not anti-religious or irreligious... Our second great principle, which flows from the first and the second, is that religion has high value but must remain in the sphere of private and personal life. It has no role to play in the politics of the country. Injecting religion into politics is against the traditions of our civilization, the canons of our Constitution and the survival of our State."

Source : Mani Shankar Aiyar, "Rajiv Gandhi in Parliament" in *Rajiv Gandhi and Parliament* (ed.) C.K. Jain, New Delhi: CBS Publishers and Distributors, 1992, p. 128.

SECULAR CULTURE

"In every village of India, in every *basti* and in every *mohalla*, there are people of different faiths, of different languages, of different cultures who live together as neighbours. Secularism is a condition of our existence. It is the essence of our tradition. Secularism and our nationhood are inseparable.

We are a multi-religious society, we are a multi-lingual society, we are a multi-cultural society, but we are not a multi-national society. We are one people, we are one nation, we are one country and we have one common citizenship."

Source: L.S. Deb, 3rd May, 1989.

SECULAR INDIA

"A patriotic Indian is a secular Indian. A nationalist Indian is a secular Indian. A disciplined Indian is secular Indian."

Source : Mani Shankar Aiyar, "Rajiv Gandhi in Parliament" in *Rajiv Gandhi and Parliament* (ed.) C.K. Jain, New Delhi: CBS Publishers and Distributors, 1992, p. 128.

SECULARISM

"...Secularism is the basis of our unity. And any force that is out of counter secularism, any communal force, any religious force, any political force that relies on communalism or on religious interests must not be allowed to use this interest to weaken the nation. We have to be very clear that on the one hand there must be full freedom for every religion, we must give every facility to allow all religions to flourish, but on the other hand we cannot allow communalism to grow. We cannot mix religion and politics which are being mixed too easily today by certain groups."

Source: L.S. Deb, 28th July, 1986, c. 354.

SELF-RELIANT INDUSTRIES

"We look for self-reliance, not autarchy. In India we today need to interact with the world market, with world industry and we realize that too much protection can be damaging to our industries. We look for improved technology, for domestic requirements, for better competitiveness, for better quality in our products, and above all, for a more efficient production process."

Source: Address to "Round Table on India", organized by the European Management Foundation, New Delhi, 15th April, 1985.

SEPARATING RELIGION AND POLITICS

"What is important is that we must separate religion and politics. They must not come together on one platform. That is something that we can do together. This question has been raised right from the time of Independence. It has been debated at the time of making the Constitution. There have been technical difficulties in actually laying down how this could be done. But the time has come now to overcome those difficulties. We cannot delay this any longer and it must be left to the genius of our people to produce a formula which will enable us to separate this."

Source: R.S. Deb, 4th March, 1987.

SKILL UPGRADATION

"Merely promoting a worker to a higher position does not automatically upgrade his skill. A large number of people are promoted by nothing is done to train for their higher callings. I find people occupying positions far above their competence levels creating innumerable problems of functioning. Training is essential; skill is essential. Training for skill upgradation is of the greatest importance. Without this we shall never be able to modernize our workforce."

Source: Free rendering of speech in Hindi at the twenty-eighth session of the Indian National Labour Conference, New Delhi, 26th November, 1985.

SOCIAL JUSTICE FOR DEMOCRACY

"When we talk of democracy, it can only survive if there is social justice to match it. Progress without social justice cannot be counted progress in a country like India."

Source: Speech while laying the foundation-stone on the Bar Council of India Bhavan, New Delhi, 19th March, 1985.

SPIRIT OF INDIA

"India is a very rich country, rich in spirituality, rich in an inner strength, in a depth which we don't find in other countries. Today, unfortunately, we only talk about material or economic benefit. This is not sufficient. For the proper nourishment of a human being much more is required than just mere economic betterment. And we must strive for this today."

Source: Speech after receiving the 1984 Dr. B.C. Roy National Award conferred posthumously on Shrimati Indira Gandhi, New Delhi, 30th April, 1985.

SPIRIT OF SACRIFICE

"Nation-building postulates the correct spirit among our people. Gandhiji, Panditji and Indiraji had explained that as long as our people do not have the spirit of sacrifice we will neither be able to make our country strong nor put it really on the path of development."

Source: Free rendering of speech in Hindi on the occasion of presenting National Bravery Awards to Children at Talkatora Stadium, New Delhi, 25th January, 1989.

SPIRITUALISM IS OUR STRENGTH

"Too often, today in the race for development and progress, our attention is attracted only towards economic or material development. This is against the ethos of India, this is against the spirit of India. India stands for total development of the human being, both material and spiritual and this is where our attention must go to."

Source: Speech at the function to mark the unveiling of the statue of Jawaharlal Nehru, Madras, 21st December, 1987.

STRENGTH OF INDIA

But the challenges are very real and we can see the tension between the new and the old strength of India, the spirituality, the inner strength that really defined India, that has kept India as India. In spite of many foreign conquests, India has not changed, it is the conqueror that has become Indian. This strength we cannot afford to lose and we will not let it weaken. We have to blend this in with modern technology, hopefully, not with modern materialism but with Indian Spirituality."

Source: Address to "Round Table on India", organized by the European Management Foundation, New Delhi, 15th April, 1985.

STRENGTHENING DEMOCRACY

"Our democracy is strong. It is very healthy and progressing rapidly. But that does not mean we can stop and rest. If democracy is to survive, if it is to be preserved, we have to defend it everyday, every minute of everyday. We have to protect it and nurture it."

Source: Free rendering of speech in Hindi on the occasion of Golden Jubilee Celebrations of U.P. Vidhan Sabha, Lucknow, 19th December, 1987.

STRENGTHENING THE PANCHAYATI RAJ SYSTEM

"After Independence, we had promised in the Constitution, to strengthen the third level of our democracy. The first and the second levels which are governed from Delhi and the State capitals, have been strengthened following several elections, and no one can weaken them. The third level, however, is weak and it affects the first two levels also, because people at the top level have become paper tigers and the structure had become hollow. This has to be set right by strengthening the Panchayati Raj Institutions."

Source: Free rendering of speech in Hindi while inaugurating the Panchayati Raj Sammelan of Northern States, New Delhi, 27th January, 1989.

STRUGGLE FOR HUMAN RIGHTS

"Across the world, slavery has been finished. Human dignity has been restored. Human rights have been restored. The final battle, the last vestige is in South Africa. This battle has to be fought not just in South Africa, it has to be fought across the world."

Source: Speech while inaugurating the Global Preparatory Meeting of Parliament for Removal of Apartheid, at New Delhi on 17th August, 1987.

STRUGGLE FOR WATER BUT MISMANAGING WATER

"Inter-State disputes, political problems coming from the usage of water or from the possible usage of water have only two or three effects. Perhaps the most important is that they waste the water while the dispute is going on. Nobody gets that water. Millions of TMC flows into the ocean, while we are quibbling about one or 0.5 TMC."

Source: Inaugural address to the National Conference of Irrigation and Water Resources, Ministers of States and Union Territories, New Delhi, 8th July, 1986.

SUBJUGATION OF SCIENTIFIC TRADITION

"Unfortunately, we went through a period of subjugation which saw the destruction of this scientific and technological tradition. It saw India reduced for a much sought after destination for knowledge and riches to an underdeveloped and developing country."

Source: Address to the Concluding session of 73rd Indian Science Congress, New Delhi, 7th January, 1986.

SYSTEMATIC SOLUTION

"As we went alone, we discovered that a managerial solution would not do. What was needed was a systematic solution...We learnt that inefficiently could only be ended by entrusting the people at the grassroots with the responsibility for their own development. We learnt that callousness could only be ended by empowering the people to send their own representatives to institutions of local self-government, by empowering the people to reject those who betray their mandate."

Source : Mani Shankar Aiyar, "Rajiv Gandhi in Parliament" in *Rajiv Gandhi and Parliament* (ed.) C.K. Jain, New Delhi: CBS Publishers and Distributors, 1992, p. 134.

TACKLING COMMUNALISM

"Communalism is perhaps the biggest danger that is afflicting our country today and we must rid the country of this. We must be seen as united in fighting this menace. There can be no compromise with communalism, especially a compromise with communalism, especially a compromise for political gains. Anybody who attempts to do that, is selling the unity and integrity of the country for his own personal gain and we cannot allow that to happen."

Source: Speech at a function held to celebrate the 125th year of publication of the *Pioneer*, New Delhi, 7th June, 1989.

TAKING INDIA TO NEW HEIGHTS

"It is not Left or Right nor Left-of-Centre nor Right-of-Centre. It is what is good for India today. Its basis was laid down by Nehru and Indira. We are shifting. But we modify their ideology with the conditions of today, that is, economic conditions in India now, improvements and progress made, financial constraints, and the situation in the world monetary and financial systems. If we balance all these, we can produce a package which will not deviate from the Congress ideology, which is dynamic and which will take India ahead."

Source : K.N. Singh, "Rajiv Gandhi – An Apostle of Peace" in *Rajiv Gandhi and Parliament* (ed.) C.K. Jain, New Delhi: CBS Publishers and Distributors, 1992, p. 159.

TECHNOLOGY AND DEVELOPMENT

"There can be but one criterion for development in the coming years: how much high technology is used in the life of our common man. Sometimes it will be used directly by him. Elsewhere, as in factories and power plants, it will be used for him. But if you do not impart proper education today, the child will not be able to use the new technology tomorrow; consequently he will be unable to become strong. Poverty will not be removed. We will not be able to break-through the shackles of backwardness."

Source: Free rending of speech in Hindi at the Asian and South Pacific Regional Educational Conference of the World's Teachers' Federation, New Delhi, 10th April, 1989.

TECHNOLOGY FOR TODAY

"There is a great deal to be done in the area of technology. Technology for the small scale industries must be developed. We must look at how we can apply technology to housing which is one of our most serious problems today. We must develop technology which will bring housing to the reach of the masses. We have to see how technology can help us in education. We must also see how education can help us with technology. We are today in a phase of development, not just in India, but the whole world, where industry and its requirements of skills are changing. The basic equipment is changing; it is not that basic any more. Today an average mechanic can learn how to repair a car by just working in a workshop for a few months. But the next generation of cars will be controlled by computers. Already the more advanced vehicles have computers on board and not just for gimmickry. They have computers on board for better fuel efficiency and to get better mileage. These things will come. They have to come. How will our mechanics repair those cars? This question, and others like it needs to be addressed."

Source: R.S. Deb, 17th December, 1985.

THE NEW EDUCATION HAS A GOAL

"The educational system must be able to develop the Indian mind, get it out of the colonial cast, make it much more outward thinking, make it more aggressive on intellectual questions. We must so mould it that the solutions that we find are found in India and not abroad."

Source: Inaugural Address to the Conference of Education Ministers of States, New Delhi, 29th August, 1985.

TOP STRONG BOTTOM WEAK

"The people at the top level were busy strengthening their own positions in politics as well as in administration and completely neglected the federal institutions."

Source: Free rendering of speech in Hindi while inaugurating the Panchayati Raj Sammelan of Northern States, New Delhi, 27th January, 1989.

TRAINING

"We also need a lot of training. Training is not a bad word, even if one is grown up. Training and learning go on throughout life. And those who cannot learn throughout life are the ones who drop by the wayside. It is only those who learn from experience, learn from the mistakes of others, learn from the work of others who are able to progress and go ahead. We must have a proper training system in the panchayats as well for building up local talent, building up local individuals, training them up to be able to cope with the problems that they face in their areas. There is no shame in going back to classes, going back to schools."

Source: Inaugural address to the 13th All India Panchayat Parishad, New Delhi, 22nd September, 1986 (Opening remarks translated from Hindi).

TRIBUTE TO TWO GANDHIANS

"And it was Smt. Soundaram Ramachandran who started Gandhigram here. It is a tribute to her vision, her work and to the ideals of Gandhiji that Gandhigram has succeeded, that Gandhigram has helped so many thousands, so many lakhs of people to improve their suffering."

Source: Speech at the Gandhi Jayanti Celebrations, Gandhigram, Tamil Nadu, 3rd October, 1988.

TRULY RESPONSIBLE ADMINISTRATION

"So, for a truly responsible administration, secularism is both a question of law and order and the response to the communal menace. You should display the ability to persuade people to abandon their base attitudes and look at things in a much broader, bigger perspective, to build on well-tried principles of good fellowship, to see ourselves as a family."

Source: Inaugural Speeches at the Workshops of District Collectors and Magistrates on Responsive Administration, Jaipur, 30th April, 1988.

TRUSTING PEOPLE

"Those who decry this as an election gimmick are precisely those whose feudal interests will be overthrown by power reaching the people. We trust the people. We have faith in people. It is the people who must determine their own destinies and the destiny of the nation.

To the people on India. Let us assure maximum democracy and maximum devolution. Let there be an end to the power-brokers. Let us give power to the people."

Source : Mani Shankar Aiyar, "Rajiv Gandhi in Parliament" in *Rajiv Gandhi and Parliament* (ed.) C.K. Jain, New Delhi: CBS Publishers and Distributors, 1992, p. 133.

21ST CENTURY INDIA

"When we talk of developing India for the 21st Century, what we are really talking about is a change in the way we think, in the way we act, to make India think boldly, think in a revolutionary manner, be assertive, be aggressive, yet not to lose the foundations of our ancient traditions and values. Our national objective is to reach the front rank of all nations."

Source: Speech after presenting the National Youth Awards 1985, New Delhi, 12th January, 1987.

UNIQUE EDUCATIONAL SYSTEM

"In Santiniketan, in your curriculum, which is unique in the sense that it builds your creativity, it builds your own expression, it allows your characters, your personalities to build. In Santiniketan, book learning is interwoven with arts, with crafts, with poetry, with dance, with drama, with songs. It is this that builds a wider perspective. You have a glorious heritage in Santiniketan, a heritage going back to Gurudev. Gurudev was, perhaps, one of the first to realize the difficulties in scientific and technological development of the human being without developing the spiritual and the inner human being. And he set out to just develop this human being. And that has been the root of this University today."

Source: Convocation address at Visva-Bharati, Santiniketan, 6th December, 1985.

UNIQUE UNIVERSITY

"Vishwabharathi cannot degenerate into a minor provincial university. It must live up to its name, bringing the world to India and taking India to the world. It cannot be done by fossilizing Rabindranath Tagore or by making Vishwabharathi into a museum. It can only be done by revitalizing the University, interpreting Tagore in modern light and making Vishwabharathi a vibrant University."

Source: Convocation address at Vishwabharathi University, Santiniketan, 7th April, 1989.

UNITED INDIA

"If the new India is to be strong, if it is to meet the challenges of the world, we must stand united and we must identify who is weakening India. We have to identify the enemies of our country, who are cutting our roots. We have to identify them and isolate them, remove them from our path. We have to remember how Gandhiji, Panditji, Indiraji and Babuji showed us that we must not deviate from our chosen path, whatever be the challenges before us, howsoever strong the pressures exerted upon us, because only by following that course will India become strong. Only that path leads to the upliftment of the poor India."

Source: Free rendering of speech in Hindi on the Occasion of the 80th Birthday of Babu Jagjivan Ram, 5th April, 1987.

UNITY AND INTEGRITY

"Nothing is more important than the unity and integrity of our nation. India is indivisible. Secularism is the bedrock of our nationhood. It implies more than tolerance. It involves an active effort for harmony. No religion preaches hatred and intolerance. Vested interests, both external and internal, are inciting and exploiting communal passions and violence to divide India. Answering communalism with communalism will only help these subversive and secessionist forces. The combined might of the people and the government will thwart their designs. There is only one India. It belongs to all of us."

Source: *Broadcast to the Nation*, 12th November, 1984.

UPHOLD THE UNITY OF INDIA

"Indira Gandhi is no more but her soul lives; India lives. India is immortal. The spirit of India is immortal. I know that the nation will recognize its responsibilities and that we shall shoulder the burden historically and with determination."

Source: Broadcast to the nation after being sworn in as Prime Minister, 31st October, 1984.

UPLIFTING WOMEN – A PRECONDITION FOR DEVELOPMENT

"As long as women have an inferior status in our society we cannot pretend that our societies are truly developing in the right direction. It is a moral blot in our societies, and perhaps also a self-inflicted economic wound. If we are to develop, and each of our country wants that development, the raising of the basic living standards of our people should be one of its major thrusts. We cannot achieve this if half of our population is not mobilized in this effort. Women are half of our population and they too must be mobilized towards contribution to national development and growth. We have to break the prejudices in the minds of men, perhaps some of this prejudice has even gone into the minds of women, and we have to break it from there as well. Education has to be the basic tool that is available to us for this; Education of values, tolerance, compassion, egalitarianism, to build in a scientific temper, so that women are able to cope with technology, whether it is in the household or whether it is at their work, a confidence in girls and a respect in boys."

Source: Inaugural Address to the Ministerial Meeting of the South Asian Association for Regional Cooperation on 'Women in Development', Shillong, 6th May, 1986.

VALUE SYSTEM IN INDIA

"What is India's special characteristic? It is that for thousands of years, we have placed certain values above material considerations."

Source: Free rendering of speech in Hindi on the occasion of Golden Jubilee Celebrations of U.P. Vidhan Sabha, Lucknow, 19th December, 1987.

VARIATIONS IN DEVOLUTION

"We have left it to State legislatures and State Governments to determine the precise contours of the responsibilities that will devolve on local bodies for the implementation of programmes. Some states will go further than others. Some variations in the degree and pattern of devolution would be justified and acceptable. But any State government which transgress the spirit of these Amendments will have to face the wrath of the people."

Source: Text of reply to the debate on the Panchayati Raj and Nagarpalika Bills, Rajya Sabha, 13th October, 1989.

WE ARE CAPABLE BUT RESTRAINT

"We are the only country who, having shown a technical capability for producing nuclear weapons, have shown a remarkable resolve not to go further down that road. For thirteen years, since Pokhran, we have demonstrated that restraint can be exercised and a technical capability does not necessarily translate into an active weapon system and its deployment. This restraint that we have shown is something that is there for the whole world to see as an example, and we have maintained it in spite of a very difficult and complex situation around us in our region."

Source: Speech at the National Defence College, 17th November, 1987.

WE ARE FOR HUMANITY DEVELOPMENT

"Too often, today in the race for development and progress, our attention is attracted only towards economic or material development. This is against the ethos of India, this is against the spirit of India. India stands for total development of the human being, both material and spiritual, and this is where our attention must go to."

Source: Speech at a function to mark the unveiling of the statue of Jawaharlar Nehru, Madras, 21st December, 1987.

WE NEED QUICK ACTION

"We must now increase efficiency, reduce cost and improve quality. Action will be needed on several fronts. We must reduce unnecessary and multiple levels in decision making and provide greater flexibility and scope for initiative."

Source: Inaugural address at the Indira Gandhi Institute of Development Research, Bombay, 28th December, 1987.

WEAK STRUCTURE OF OUR DEMOCRACY

"Till now, there have been weakness in the structure of our democracy because, although the superstructure is strong, the foundation has been weak."

Source: L.S. Deb, 15th May, 1989.

WHERE ARE HARIJANS IN PANCHAYATS?

"Another weak point which I have noticed is our Panchayati Raj set-up. Think for yourselves. When parliamentary elections are held, many Scheduled Caste MPs are elected. Harijans get elected to the Vidhan Sabhas. But when elections are held for the Gram Sabha, the Block Samiti, or the Zilla Parishad, how many Harijans get in? How many are elected to these bodies? Just think, how many become chairmen? Count and you see the weakness. There is hardly any representation. This has to be set right today because as long as we do not rectify the situation at this level, no amount of noise at higher level will be of any use."

Source: Free rendering of speech in Hindi after laying the foundation stone of Dr. Ambedkar University, Lucknow, 14th April, 1989.

WHERE IS WOMEN IN GOVERNANCE?

"First, women constitute half the population and are involved in rather more than half the economic life of rural India. However, to our shame, their share of assets and income is much less than their share of the population but the toil and sweat imposed upon them is rather more than half."

Source: L.S. Deb, 15th May, 1989.

WOMEN TO BE EMPOWERED

"A society's progress can really be judged by how well half our society progresses. And if they are to progress fast, half the talent, half the energy cannot be ignored. Women must be allowed full freedom of action and movement. Women are equal in every way, whether in spiritual urges or in political ideals. Historically, in the matter of sacrifices, in heroism, there have been no differences just because of sex. Women have risen to the highest levels of sacrifice, the highest levels of heroism. This is evident from all our freedom struggles."

Source: Inaugural address at the Conference of Non-aligned and other Developing countries on the Role of Women in Development, New Delhi, 10th April, 1985.

WOMEN UNDER-REPRESENTED

"We have also seen that women are under-represented in Panchayati Raj Institutions. This is most unfortunate as it is women who undertake much more than half the economic activities in rural India. It is women to whom is entrusted the welfare and, often, the finances of the household. It is the women of rural India who are the main repository of India's great cultural traditions, of the moral values which are fundamental to the survival and efflorescence of our civilization."

Source: Speech at the Conference of Chief Ministers on Panchayati Raj, New Delhi, 5th May, 1989.

WOMEN WITH MORAL STRENGTH

"It is the women of India, in their role as grandmothers and mothers, who have been the repository of India's ancient culture and traditions. It is to them that is entrusted the responsibility of transmitting to the next generation the quintessential values, standards and ideals which have enabled our civilization to survive and flourish without a break despite vicissitudes of many kinds. It is the strength of moral character which women will bring to the panchayats."

Source: L.S. Deb, 15th May, 1989.

WORK FOR UNITY

"We will never let India be divided. We will see that these forces are fought in every way, whether the opposition comes along with us or does not come along with us. We are prepared to fight alone. We are prepared to confront them. Whenever such an occasion has come, the Congress has stood firm and exerted itself fully. The Congress has never backed out of such a struggle, whatever the sacrifices needed. We have never retreated and today also we are not going to retreat."

Source: Free rendering of speech in Hindi after laying the foundation stone of Dr. Ambedkar University, Lucknow, 14th April, 1989.

Section – II

A FREE THINKER

"Rajiv Gandhi was not an intellectual or a scholar with any claim of erudition or extraordinary artistic accomplishments. But, he was intensely human, warm-hearted, compassionate, courteous and ever-smiling. Here was a man without fear, and with malice and ill-will against none! A free thinker, uninhibited by any dogma or narrow-mindedness, he was a firm believer in open society. He possessed great common sense to realize that it is not by breaking up the mould of the past that changes in society could be made. He recognized that some institutions tend to corrupt society but to mould them to the changing needs of society, one has to go slow by viewing the whole spectrum of the past in perspective. To meet the socio-economic challenges of his time he thought that his grandfather Nehru's socio-economic model was still relevant."

Source: S.M.H. Burney, "Rajiv Gandhi – An Assessment" in *Rajiv Gandhi and Parliament* (ed.) C.K. Jain, New Delhi: CBS Publishers and Distributors, 1992.

A MAN WHO STOOD TALL

"In the first few shocking days after the 21st of May 1991 it was difficult to accept the fact that Rajiv Gandhi's youthful presence would not be with us—a man who stood tall, not only amongst the men of political life in India, but also amongst the statesmen of the world. This was something out of the ordinary. We are too close to the time to be able to have a perspective of the personality of Rajiv Gandhi in world affairs. The profound respect and affection which the leaders of the world had for him and still have, is something to be seen to be believed."

Source: P.V. Narasimha Rao, "Rajiv Gandhi and his Perspective" in *Rajiv Gandhi and Parliament* (ed.) C.K. Jain, New Delhi: CBS Publishers and Distributors, 1992.

A NEW ERA

"Rajiv Gandhi's short but brilliant political life has left its indelible mark on the polity of our times. The era of Rajiv Gandhi was the era of great activity and excitement, of new ideas and of experimentation. He brought the freshness and vigour of youth in the administration of the country and generated a whole new set of ideas, whose expression is being seen today and will be evident for man years into the future."

Source: P.V. Narasimha Rao, "Rajiv Gandhi and his Perspective" in *Rajiv Gandhi and Parliament* (ed.) C.K. Jain, New Delhi: CBS Publishers and Distributors, 1992.

A STATESMAN

"Rajiv Gandhi's was a statesman among statesmen, a farmer among farmers, a poor person among the poor people and a child among the children. This was the kind of adaptability that he had learnt within that very short period. We have lost a person who was a class by himself. One could not replicate Rajiv Gandhi. This is a fact with which both his friends and opponents will have to agree. History will have to record this as an indelible fact."

Source: P.V. Narasimha Rao, "Rajiv Gandhi and his Perspective" in *Rajiv Gandhi and Parliament* (ed.) C.K. Jain, New Delhi: CBS Publishers and Distributors, 1992.

AN INNOVATIVE PARLIAMENTARIAN

"Rajiv was an able Parliamentarian. He had shown a great respect for and an abiding faith in parliamentary democracy. He worked ceaselessly to strengthen the roots of parliamentary system in India. He believed that through this system alone the fruits of freedom can be made available to the people at large. In Parliament his style of functioning was often unconventional. Despite enjoying more than three-fourth majority in the Lok Sabha, he never functioned arbitrarily as leader of possible, to carry the Opposition along with him in all important matters under consideration of the House. He welcomed criticism not only from the Opposition but gave even his own party members the right to seek clarifications and the right to offer constructive criticism on government policies. He built up the parliamentary traditions of restraint and moderation, dignity and decorum. While dealing with the Opposition, he found himself at ease as his answers and explanations were direct and frank."

Source: K.N. Singh, "Rajiv Gandhi – An Apostle of Peace" in *Rajiv Gandhi and Parliament* (ed.) C.K. Jain, New Delhi: CBS Publishers and Distributors, 1992.

AN OUTSTANDING DEMOCRAT

"An analytical study of the speeches of Rajiv Gandhi in Parliament and outside proves that firstly, he was a democrat, secondly, he had slowly developed the tact and skill of a good parliamentarian and thirdly, instead of the Parliamentary Cabinet system he preferred a Parliamentary Presidential system of government. He could not do what he wanted to do, because he was not able to pick up and develop instruments of his choice—whether persons or systems. He could not opt for Presidential system where his performance would have been far better, rather spectacular, and he could not build a team wedded to his ideals and high principles; rather the persons he had chosen, ditched him."

Source: Siddheshwar Prasad, "Rajiv Gandhi as a Parliamentarian" in *Rajiv Gandhi and Parliament* (ed.) C.K. Jain, New Delhi: CBS Publishers and Distributors, 1992.

BETRAYAL TOLERATED

"I never found him either resentful or peevish. He did not deem it fit to be vengeful even during the bitterest phase of the betrayal by some of his most trusted colleagues or nearest advisers. Even the prolonged and painful campaign of betrayal by some of his colleagues and some newspapers and the newsmen, did not provoke him into expressions of hatred or contempt."

Source: N.G. Ranga, "India's Rajivji" in *Rajiv Gandhi and Parliament* (ed.) C.K. Jain, New Delhi: CBS Publishers and Distributors, 1992.

COMMITTED FOR DECENTRALIZATION

"His five years as Prime Minister were a period of modernization, economic growth and social transformation. His commitment to decentralization of administration was total. He was convinced that a nation of India's size having more than 85 million people could not be governed properly by sitting at Delhi and the State capitals. A few Ministers sitting in Delhi and State capitals would not be able to understand the innumerable problems faced by various sections of the Indian people."

Source: A.K. Antony, "Rajiv Gandhi – A Man of Action" in *Rajiv Gandhi and Parliament* (ed.) C.K. Jain, New Delhi: CBS Publishers and Distributors, 1992.

CONCERN FOR DEPRESSED CLASS

"Shri Rajiv Gandhi's deep commitment to the cause of the downtrodden and the deprived people did not remain confined to India but extended far beyond the national frontiers. He was concerned about the people of Africa and Asia. He was instrumental in setting up of the AFRICA Fund. He was against the practice of *apartheid* and had raised his voice against *Zionism.*"

Source: Najma Heptulla, "Rajiv Gandhi As I Knew Him" in *Rajiv Gandhi and Parliament* (ed.) C.K. Jain, New Delhi: CBS Publishers and Distributors, 1992.

CONSTITUTIONAL REFORMER

"As we have seen, Shri Rajiv Gandhi was verily committed to the Constitution, to the Parliament and ultimately to the people. Truly, a constitutional reformer, he went about his task with youthful vigour and enthusiasm. Ever undaunted by challenges and reverses he strove hard to achieve the lofty goals he had set before himself. What he wanted of course was to prepare the nation for the next century. He adopted the right means to arrive at the right conclusions and ends. He was willing to learn from others, from experience. He showed a rare skill in carrying the people and the Parliament with him."

Source: C.K. Jain, "Rajiv Gandhi – His Role as a Constitutional Reformer" in *Rajiv Gandhi and Parliament* (ed.) C.K. Jain, New Delhi: CBS Publishers and Distributors, 1992.

DECENCY AND FAIR PLAY

"Rajiv Gandhi, naturally, took his own time to get used to the rough and tumble of political life in India. He seemed to have learnt much during the 18 months he was in the Opposition when, tragically, his life was cut short by a thoughtless fanatic. His sense of decency and fair play remained, by and large, one of his admirable qualities."

Source: Prem Bhatia, "Rajiv Gandhi – In and Outside Parliament" in *Rajiv Gandhi and Parliament* (ed.) C.K. Jain, New Delhi: CBS Publishers and Distributors, 1992.

DEEP COMMITMENT IN INTERNATIONAL AFFAIRS

"An outstanding quality of Rajiv Gandhi was his keen interest in international affairs. Aware of the changing global equations, it was his firm belief that India had to play an active role for securing justice. He was keen that India plays a major role in the world youth movement and that our younger generation besides being conscious of its national duties, develops an international outlook."

Source: Anand Sharma, "Memories of Rajiv Gandhi" in *Rajiv Gandhi and Parliament* (ed.) C.K. Jain, New Delhi: CBS Publishers and Distributors, 1992.

DETERMINED ENDEAVOUR

"Shri Rajiv Gandhi's five years as Prime Minister were marked by a determined endeavour towards rapid modernization, economic growth and sensitive, yet decisive handling of myriad problems. He was ever conscious of the need to propel India towards the Third Millennium as a strong, united, self-sufficient and modern nation."

Source: C.K. Jain, "Rajiv Gandhi – His Role as a Constitutional Reformer" in *Rajiv Gandhi and Parliament* (ed.) C.K. Jain, New Delhi: CBS Publishers and Distributors, 1992.

EMINENT PARLIAMENTARIAN

"A good parliamentarian should, of course, have the capacity to speak fluently and with clarity during discussions and debates and Rajiv Gandhi was not found wanting in this regard. On all the occasions when he spoke in Parliament, he displayed these qualities in an abundant measure, whether he spoke in English or in Hindi. We cannot forget the very able way in which he managed the debate on the Budget proposals when he was holding the finance portfolio.

Rajiv Gandhi was well known for his affable nature, courtesy, cordiality and candidness. These qualities served him in good stead in his parliamentary behaviour. It cannot be denied that these qualities contribute to the stature and effectiveness of every Parliamentarian. Rajiv Gandhi's success as Parliamentarian was at least partly, due to these personal qualities. There were many occasions when vituperative personal attacks were made against him during the debates and he always kept his cool and refused to be provoked. This attitude often disarmed his critics."

Source: Shri S.B. Chavan, "Rajiv Gandhi as a Parliamentarian" in *Rajiv Gandhi and Parliament* (ed.) C.K. Jain, New Delhi: CBS Publishers and Distributors, 1992.

FORESIGHTED VISIONARY

"Shri Rajiv Gandhi was a visionary symbolizing the future. He represented hope, aspiration and enthusiasm of the youth. His thoughts were clear; his words sincere, his deeds purposeful and his principles firm. He cared for the poor, he cared for the deprived; in fact, and he cared for every section of our society. He wanted India to develop in every way taking full advantage of the advances in modern science and technology and thus emerge as a strong and internationally competitive economy."

Source: Manmohan Singh, "Rajiv Gandhi – A Visionary" in *Rajiv Gandhi and Parliament* (ed.) C.K. Jain, New Delhi: CBS Publishers and Distributors, 1992.

FORTHRIGHTNESS

"His readiness to face to Motion of No-Confidence and Adjournment Motions and all other crucial debates on the floor of the House, was marked by his rare forthrightness, and his replies were prompt, sharp, witty and be-fitting. The orientation to the functioning of various Consultative Committees, attached to the Ministries was also remarkable. He wanted these Committees to study specific topics in-depth and not to deal with trivial matters."

Source: N.C. Parashar, "Rajiv Gandhi as a Parliamentarian" in *Rajiv Gandhi and Parliament* (ed.) C.K. Jain, New Delhi: CBS Publishers and Distributors, 1992.

GAVE NEW IMPETUS TO SAARC

"The Foreign Policy of Rajiv Gandhi was not only preoccupied with the larger affairs of the world but also with the hard and complex problems of the neighbourhood. In South Asia, without compromising on basic principles and national interests, he strove for reconciliation friendship and cooperation. He tried to give a new impetus to SAARC."

Source: K.R. Narayanan, "The Foreign Policy of Rajiv Gandhi" in *Rajiv Gandhi and Parliament* (ed.) C.K. Jain, New Delhi: CBS Publishers and Distributors, 1992.

GEM AMONG THE JEWELS

"He moved among the masses fearlessly in every corner of the country and even in Sri Lanka in spite of attempts on his life at Raj Ghat and in Sri Lanka. He represented the cause of the Third World and made the Non-Aligned Movement so powerful that the capitalist countries could not succeed in the United Nations in pursuing their vested interests during his Prime Ministership. Vested interests in the country and in the outside world were so apprehensive of his capabilities that their conspirators eliminated the angel of peace and prosperity and the crusader of the poor masses and underdeveloped nations of the world. Shri Rajiv Gandhi was the Gem among the Jewels of crusaders."

Source: Ranbir Singh, "Shri Rajiv Gandhi – The Gem Among the Jewels" in *Rajiv Gandhi and Parliament* (ed.) C.K. Jain, New Delhi: CBS Publishers and Distributors, 1992.

GOOD LISTENER

"Rajiv would never come to the House without sufficient preparations. Every speech he made is a rich source of facts and figures to the research scholars on the functioning of Parliament. He always wanted to be sure on facts and his arguments were unassailable. When he was the Prime Minister he made every effort to attend the meetings of Consultative Committees of Departments attached to him. He would sit through and listen patiently to the views of members. His very presence in such meeting compelled the members to study the subject and make meaningful contribution. More emphasis was laid on study and discussion on policy issues in these meetings rather than discussion on the written questions of members about various local problems and the Department's written briefs on them."

Source: P.J. Kurien, "Rajiv Gandhi – A Parliamentarian Par Excellence" in *Rajiv Gandhi and Parliament* (ed.) C.K. Jain, New Delhi: CBS Publishers and Distributors, 1992.

GREAT SON OF INDIA

"This great son of India will long be remembered for his patriotic fervour, his compassion to the poor and the needy, his unmatched capacity to handle men and matters, his quick grasp, his sincerity of purpose and his efforts to raise the standard of living of the people and to resolve the problems of the nation."

Source: S.M. Krishna, "Rajiv Gandhi: An Indomitable Personality" in *Rajiv Gandhi and Parliament* (ed.) C.K. Jain, New Delhi: CBS Publishers and Distributors, 1992.

HIS GREATEST CONTRIBUTION

"Perhaps Rajiv Gandhi's greatest contribution was in his efforts to free the Indian people from bureaucratic oppression and the hold of local anti-social elements. He felt that if parliamentary democracy was to succeed in India the voter had to be educated, relieved of unhealthy pressures and made self-reliant."

Source: Dinesh Singh, "Rajiv Gandhi – As a Parliamentarian" in *Rajiv Gandhi and Parliament* (ed.) C.K. Jain, New Delhi: CBS Publishers and Distributors, 1992.

IN SUPPORT OF PEOPLES STRUGGLE

"During a period when India was called to play an important role in the international arena, given its non-aligned foreign policy and support for national liberation struggles in the Third World, Rajiv Gandhi utilized this opportunity to establish a direct rapport with various world leaders. The Delhi Declaration, after Mikhail Gorbachev's visit to India and the Belgrade Summit of the NAM were some of the important landmarks during his tenure. The galaxy of leaders from across the world who had turned up at the funeral of Shri Gandhi was a reminder of the sterling role that India had played in support of the struggling peoples of South Africa, Palestine, Namibia, Kampuchea, Afghanistan etc.

One may agree or disagree with the view that Shri Gandhi's interventions in the debates in Parliament, both as Prime Minister and later as Leader of the Opposition were precise and to the point. However, his contribution to Parliament has left its own imprint.

Though the enemies of the country have killed him, Shri Gandhi's memory will always remain."

Source: Harikishan Singh Surjeet, "Rajiv Gandhi and the Indian Parliament" in *Rajiv Gandhi and Parliament* (ed.) C.K. Jain, New Delhi: CBS Publishers and Distributors, 1992.

INSIGHT

"Rajivji brought to the Parliament a new dynamism and liveliness. His sharp wit and humour provided the much needed relief during heated debates. He had in-depth knowledge on most of the subjects and was very much at home, irrespective of the topic of discussion. He made the most complex tasks look simple by his insight, perception, confidence and enthusiasm that were an inseparable part of him. He inspired great confidence in all those who were associated with him by effortlessly passing on to them all these qualities."

Source: Ahmed M. Patel, "Rajiv Gandhi – Leader with Compassion" in *Rajiv Gandhi and Parliament* (ed.) C.K. Jain, New Delhi: CBS Publishers and Distributors, 1992.

INTERNATIONAL STATESMAN

"Rajiv Gandhi would be remembered as a great international statesman. He conceived of a new world order of his own style, a world beyond war, nations without barriers and peoples in peace and harmony. Innately, he was a man of peace, with his own interior life and inner self. It is because of this inner strength, he was very much at ease in all capitals of the world he visited, or the people he met, whether in Europe, Asia or Africa. All over the world, he won the hearts of the people with his charm, his open and frank style, and with his ready sense of humour which never deserted him even in times of great pressures and crises. In the international arena, he was a campaigner seeking to set right the ills that he saw. His philosophy was to move the mental hurdles between nations so that a new world order would be established, with all peoples living in peace and harmony with each other, individually and socially. He was a champion of the cause of the oppressed peoples in their struggle to direct their own destinies and stood up for tolerance and co-existence among nations where differences would be resolved by peaceful means. At various international fora, and during his numerous visits abroad, Rajiv Gandhi tried to secure a place for India to play a constructive role in sorting out various international issues."

Source: Janak Raj Gupta, "Rajiv Gandhi – As I Knew Him" in *Rajiv Gandhi and Parliament* (ed.) C.K. Jain, New Delhi: CBS Publishers and Distributors, 1992.

INVINCIBLE FOR THE OPPOSITION

"Indian politics got the youngest ever Prime Minister in Rajiv Gandhi. This phenomenon attracted attention the world over. But this youngest of all the proceeding Prime Ministers—a person having little experience as a Parliamentarian and administrator—had a historic legacy, the preservation and protection of which was his cherished dream. More than this, his winsome smile, charm and decency were his valuable personal assets. That is why everyone was impressed by the maiden speech delivered by Shri Rajiv Gandhi in the Lok Sabha as Prime Minister, and they said that it was excellent. The House was spellbound when he spoke for half-an-hour in reply to the debate on the Motion of Thanks to the President's Address. He impressed everyone with his sharp and pointed replies to the queries of the Opposition members. In fact, it was a pleasant surprise for the members. That day, a senior Opposition member, while talking to me, conceded that Rajiv Gandhi's maiden performance was extremely impressive and he could not conceal his feeling that Rajiv Gandhi would prove to be invincible for the Opposition."

Source: Satyendra Narayan Sinha, "Shri Rajiv Gandhi – A Well-versed Parliamentarian" in *Rajiv Gandhi and Parliament* (ed.) C.K. Jain, New Delhi: CBS Publishers and Distributors, 1992.

LEADER OF THE THIRD WORLD

"He was perhaps the most popular leader of the Third World Countries. This was because of his determined efforts towards modernization. Whether it was the Non-Aligned Meeting, the Commonwealth Conference, the AFRICA Fund or the South-South Dialogue, he carried with him the point-of-view of the developing countries."

Source: S.Z. Qasim, "Rajiv Gandhi and High Technology" in *Rajiv Gandhi and Parliament* (ed.) C.K. Jain, New Delhi: CBS Publishers and Distributors, 1992.

LEFT ON INTELLIGIBLE MARK

"Of the many great personalities that strode the halls of India's Parliament, only a few had so quickly made such an impact as Rajiv Gandhi. Before his mother's tragic death, few had anticipated that this ever-polite and gracious young man would be able to make so great a mark in the Parliament of world's largest democracy. Besides the great inheritance from both his mother and father who had, in their times, been great parliamentarians, and from his grandfather, Jawaharlal Nehru, Rajiv in his few short years made a unique and unforgettable impact and impression."

Source: Madhavrao Scindia, "Rajiv and Parliament" in *Rajiv Gandhi and Parliament* (ed.) C.K. Jain, New Delhi: CBS Publishers and Distributors, 1992.

MODERN NATIONAL ARCHITECT

"Rajiv had a sound perception of building a modern India. He realized early that India could never step into the 21st century unless it inducted, on a massive scale, science and technology, accepted modern methods of management and opened up the economy to competition."

Source: R. Vijaya Bhaskara Reddy, "Rajiv Gandhi – A Born Leader" in *Rajiv Gandhi and Parliament* (ed.) C.K. Jain, New Delhi: CBS Publishers and Distributors, 1992.

"Listening to him was always a pleasure. He was eloquent but never pompous, tough but always gentle, an idealist, but still a realist. Rajiv Gandhi derived his greatness from and through his actions in Parliament and those actions; he in turn added his unique contribution to the greatness of our Parliamentary institution. He was in a real sense, a product of Parliament and also equally contributed to its greatness. His words made everyone accept the adage that the number of years alone does not make a person old; it is knowledge and inner refinement which makes it. He never took anything for granted or considered Parliament less important because of his party's massive majority in the House. He always made elaborate preparations before coming to the House and took the nation into confidence through the Parliament on all issues of national and international importance. How deeply committed he was to the cause of parliamentary democracy can be seen from the fact that it was he who was instrumental in the passing of some momentous and historical pieces of legislation, such as lowering of the voting age to 18 and the anti-defection bill. These legislations, needless to say, contributed in no small measure towards magnifying the ambit of our democratic polity and providing wholesome parameters to political dynamics."

Source: Shivraj V. Patil, "Remembering Rajiv" in *Rajiv Gandhi and Parliament* (ed.) C.K. Jain, New Delhi: CBS Publishers and Distributors, 1992.

NEW STYLE OF CONFRONTATION

"Rajiv Gandhi had not prepared himself for parliamentary life when he was catapulted into the seat of Prime Minister and the Leader of the House in Lok Sabha. Nor had he quite mastered the art of parliamentary practice when he was martyred last year. Partly because of this and partly because of his straightforward nature, Rajiv Gandhi evolved a style of his own to deal with the difficult problems of one of the most complex Parliaments of the world, i.e. Parliament of India. He faced questions squarely and replied fearlessly. There was no duplicity in his statements; no ambiguity either. He dealt with the Opposition in the same manner. Always he took the bull by the horns. It was not an easy way of dealing with those opposed to him, but Rajiv Gandhi was concerned about the issues and not personalities. About the issues, he went about passionately in dealing with them. Whether in the Government as Prime Minister or as Leader of the Opposition when out of it, Rajiv Gandhi's emphasis on issues did not change his style of confrontation."

Source: Dinesh Singh, "Rajiv Gandhi – As a Parliamentarian" in *Rajiv Gandhi and Parliament* (ed.) C.K. Jain, New Delhi: CBS Publishers and Distributors, 1992.

NON-VIOLENCE

"Rajiv Gandhi's style of functioning was guided by non-violence based on constitutionalism. His approach to the solution of all problems, national or international, was pragmatic, dynamic, yet humane and non-violent. His belief in non-violence was not borne out of fear, but from an exceptional courage of conviction. For a man whose life was under constant threat, he revealed no anxiety or fear for his personal safety. He neither gave vent to his anger at any time, nor did he bear any grudge against anybody. If he wanted to avenge an adversary, it was always with love and affection. To all knotty problems, he sought solutions not by the use of force, but through discussion and dialogue."

Source: Janak Raj Gupta, "Rajiv Gandhi – As I Knew Him" in *Rajiv Gandhi and Parliament* (ed.) C.K. Jain, New Delhi: CBS Publishers and Distributors, 1992.

PRINCE AMONG THE POLITICIANS

"As a person, Rajiv Gandhi was not merely the Prime Minister of this country and President of the Indian National Congress; he was much more. If we think about him dispassionately, our heart begins to throb, our voice gets chocked and the vision gets blurred. Rajiv Gandhi was not only the President of the largest party and the Prime Minister of the biggest democracy in the world but, despite his young age, he was also a fully matured human being and because of his qualities of head and heart and by his words and deeds, he was truly a prince among the politicians of this extraordinarily beautiful world."

Source: Sujrendra Vikram, "Rajiv Gandhi - A Star in the Galaxy of Incarnates" in *Rajiv Gandhi and Parliament* (ed.) C.K. Jain, New Delhi: CBS Publishers and Distributors, 1992.

RARE AMONG RAREST

"The very name of Rajiv Gandhi evokes images of charm, freshness, youth, vigour, hope, dynamism, modernity and above all humanity. Shri Rajiv Gandhi had all these qualities in abundance which he placed at the service of the nation."

Source: Manmohan Singh, "Rajiv Gandhi – A Visionary" in *Rajiv Gandhi and Parliament* (ed.) C.K. Jain, New Delhi: CBS Publishers and Distributors, 1992.

RIGHT SUCCESSOR

"Shri Rajiv Gandhi entered politics with very little experience. Though the glory of his grandfather and his mother was with him, yet it was generally cited by his detractors only to show how unfit Shri Rajiv Gandhi was to be their successor in politics. He chose his own path. He presented his programme with a call to march into the twenty-first century with modernization and advancement in the field of science and technology. His programme was quite different from the previous Prime Minister's programmes."

Source: Jagdish Prasad Chaturvedi, "Shri Rajiv Gandhi – An Assessment" in *Rajiv Gandhi and Parliament* (ed.) C.K. Jain, New Delhi: CBS Publishers and Distributors, 1992.

SHADOW CABINET

"Rajiv Gandhi also introduced a new style of functioning for the Congress Party in Parliament. He wanted his party members to be well informed and well prepared. Towards this end he revitalized parliamentary party committees and insisted on the party committees concerned with various Ministries to meet regularly and study problems connected with their areas of interest. Reports were to be sent to him regularly so that he would be kept informed and the members would know that their contribution was being noted. When out of power, Rajiv Gandhi set up a committee of his senior colleagues as a kind of 'shadow cabinet' as in Britain."

Source: Dinesh Singh, "Rajiv Gandhi – As a Parliamentarian" in *Rajiv Gandhi and Parliament* (ed.) C.K. Jain, New Delhi: CBS Publishers and Distributors, 1992.

STATESMAN OF EXCELLENT CALIBRE

"Rajiv Gandhi began his tenure on a note of cooperation and accommodation in every sphere of political and administrative life. He heralded the beginning of a new style of functioning and soon proved himself to be a leader and a statesman of excellent calibre. He proved himself to be an apostle of peace and a crusader for justice. His policy of reconciliation and wholesome pragmatism earned him so much acclaim that even his bitterest critics in the media and politics went on record for having praised his style of functioning."

Source: K.N. Singh, "Rajiv Gandhi – An Apostle of Peace" in *Rajiv Gandhi and Parliament* (ed.) C.K. Jain, New Delhi: CBS Publishers and Distributors, 1992.

STOOD FOR HIGH PRINCIPLES

"Rajiv stood for high principles, discipline and lofty ideals. He displayed a rare sense of social awareness and concern for public welfare. He was a born leader. I thought who would reorganize and revitalize the party, break the nexus between political parties and vested interests and wage relentless war against all those who exploited the poor and the down-trodden in the name of caste and religion."

Source: R. Vijaya Bhaskara Reddy, "Rajiv Gandhi – A Born Leader" in *Rajiv Gandhi and Parliament* (ed.) C.K. Jain, New Delhi: CBS Publishers and Distributors, 1992.

STOOD FOR SECULARISM

"Shri Rajiv Gandhi always fought for communal harmony and national unity. He was firm like rock; an enemy of fundamentalism, he took all the steps to defeat communal forces and to uphold the principles of democratic secularism. He had expressed his dream of India, "I have nursed a dream, a dream of the great Indian people marching confidently into the future. I dream of an India that excels itself. Together, we can fulfil that dream". For the unity of the country, he felt, "If I need to shed my blood for keeping the country united, I will not hesitate to do so." Ultimately, he gave his life for the unity and integrity of our country."

Source: B. Satyanarayan Reddy, "Shri Rajiv Gandhi – A Dynamic Leader" in *Rajiv Gandhi and Parliament* (ed.) C.K. Jain, New Delhi: CBS Publishers and Distributors, 1992.

TRUE HEIR OF NEHRU

"It is my personal impression that Rajiv Gandhi had become the true heir of Jawaharlal's vision. I don't know when and where Rajivji studied the culture of India in the light of its history or when the concept of 'Unity in Diversity' made itself clear to him, but of one thing I am sure: he acknowledged the fact that in spite of the diversity, in spite of its flowers varied with colours and fragrances, India is a huge garden; it is a compact unit. He was not a mere spectator looking from outside, but he, who imbibed the essence of culture and Jawaharlal's vision, was an active participant in the process of promoting the concept of 'Unity in Diversity'. His humanism was very much evident when he talked about the division of our country on the basis of religion, caste and creed. Whenever he talked about the atrocities on Harijans, any communal party's fascism, communal riots, South Africa, Sri Lanka or the Palestine problem, one could easily understand the directions of his thought."

Source: Shakeelur Rehman, "Rajiv Gandhi – Vision and Personality" in *Rajiv Gandhi and Parliament* (ed.) C.K. Jain, New Delhi: CBS Publishers and Distributors, 1992.

WORLD LEADER

"Rajiv Gandhi was able to become a World Leader at a comparatively young age. His role to make SARRC a major instrument in defusing tension and promoting co-operation between the member countries will ever be remembered. His bold initiative to find out a solution to the border problems with China also will be remembered by generations of Indians."

Source: A.K. Antony, "Rajiv Gandhi – A Man of Action" in *Rajiv Gandhi and Parliament* (ed.) C.K. Jain, New Delhi: CBS Publishers and Distributors, 1992.

YOUNGEST LEADER

"Rajiv was the country's youngest Prime Minister and also the youngest Leader of the Opposition. He was also the youngest former Prime Minister to die. He was in politics only for ten years but in or out of power, his commitment throughout was to the country and to the people."

Source: Satya Prakash Malaviya, "Rajiv Gandhi – As I had known Him" in *Rajiv Gandhi and Parliament* (ed.) C.K. Jain, New Delhi: CBS Publishers and Distributors, 1992.